D0866834

The Unknown Soldier and His Wife

The UNKNOWN SOLDIER and HIS WIFE

Peter Ustinov

RANDOM HOUSE • NEW YORK

 Published in New York by Random House, Inc., and simultaneously in Toronto, Canada, by Random House of Canada Limited.

Photographs by courtesy of Freidman-Abeles
Library of Congress Catalog Card Number: 67-31084
Manufactured in the United States of America

THE UNKNOWN SOLDIER AND HIS WIFE *was first presented on July 6, 1967, by Alexander H. Cohen at the Vivian Beaumont Theatre, Lincoln Center, New York City, with the following cast:*

(In order of appearance)

SERGEANT	W. B. Brydon
35914	Don Scardino
GENERAL	Brian Bedford
REBEL	James Storm
WIFE	Melissa C. Murphy
ARCHBISHOP	Howard DaSilva
14768	Andrew Johns
71696	William Dolive
THE UNKNOWN SOLDIER	Christopher Walken
94343	Palmer Deane
ENEMY LEADER	Alan Mixon
INVENTOR	Bob Dishy
WOMAN	Nancy Reardon
REINFORCEMENTS	Gary Barton
	B. J. DeSimone
	Tom Fuccello
	Larry Swanson

Directed by John Dexter
Music by David Shire
Scenery and Costumes by Motley
Lighting by Jules Fisher
Associate Producer Hildy Parks
Production Supervisor Jerry Adler

The Unknown Soldier and His Wife

A NOTE ON THE PRODUCTION

The first performance of this play took place on the thrust stage of the Vivian Beaumont Theatre, and a certain amount of visual changes took place when it was transferred to a more conventional theatre on Broadway. The stage directions have been left as much as possible in their original form, as designed for a curtainless arena; but if the reader should notice one or two anomolies amongst them, he is begged to excuse them, and to make a few unusual demands on his imagination.

On a technical level the play was intended as an exercise for the imagination of actors and director, a challenge which Mr. John Dexter and his talented team of performers accepted immediately to our common advantage. It is in this spirit that the text is submitted for the reader's indulgence.

FIRST ACT OF WAR

The curtain rises on a stage bare but for a tomb. There are a couple of television cameras, protected by shiny plastic covers against the rain. Soldiers, at ease, stand with their backs to the audience. They are wearing camouflage gas-capes. The setting and the costuming are left to the discretion of the director throughout, the only admonition of the author being that the action should be as fluid and theatrical as possible. Any excess of the imagination is an error on the right side.

A new arrival makes his way to the front of the stage. He carries a bugle. A soldier at the end of the line approaches the newcomer purposefully. He is the SERGEANT.

SERGEANT Bugler, you're late.

BUGLER (*Who will later be known as* 35914) *Sorry,* Sar'nt. See, owing to the rain—

SERGEANT I don't want to hear no shudderin' excuses. The plungin' facts speak for themselves, got me? You're on a charge.

BUGLER Yes, Sar'nt.

SERGEANT Don't you answer back, or I'll make it stiflin' for you!

BUGLER Sar'nt.

SERGEANT Now. On the signal bein' given from the television booth up there, you play what?

BUGLER Last Post.

SERGEANT Last Post what?

BUGLER *The* Last Post.

SERGEANT *The* Last Post what? (*Pause; the* BUGLER *is perplexed*) Bugler, I am waitin'. *The* Last Post what?

BUGLER (*Tentative*) *The* Last Post, Sar'nt?

SERGEANT That's better. Now, when I raise my right hand in this manner here, you will raise your bugle to what?

BUGLER My lips, Sar'nt.

SERGEANT Now we're getting somewhere at last. You will then play the aforesaid piece of music in a manner appropriate to what type of occasion?

BUGLER Sad occasion, Sar'nt.

SERGEANT Dodderin' dummit—you don't bleedin' remember, do you? I'll try again. What type of occasion?

BUGLER Melancholic occasion, Sar'nt?

SERGEANT One more fancy word out of you, and I'll put you under arrest! Do I convey my meanin'?

BUGLER Yes, Sar'nt.

SERGEANT As you were, then. We'll try again. What manner of occasion? (*Silence. The* SERGEANT *shouts*) A solemn occasion, you half-cock! (*He inclines his head as though tuning a delicate instrument*) Appropriate to what?

BUGLER A solemn occasion, Sar'nt.

SERGEANT What is appropriate to a solemn occasion, then?

BUGLER The way I play my bugle, Sar'nt.

SERGEANT The way you play what on your bugle, Bugler?

BUGLER The Last Post, Sar'nt.

SERGEANT Got that in yer 'ead, have you?

BUGLER Yes, Sar'nt.

SERGEANT You're not very bright, are you?

BUGLER No, Sar'nt.

SERGEANT Well, we can't all be bright, can we?

BUGLER No, Sar'nt.

SERGEANT That's better. At ease. As you were! At ease. As you were! (*The* GENERAL *walks over. The* SERGEANT *comes to a thunderous attention*) Bugler present and correct, sah!

GENERAL Good. Good. Try and keep the noise down.

SERGEANT I impressed that on the bugler, sir.

GENERAL (*With a sad, occasional smile*) Good man. You will start playing the Last Post when the Sergeant here gives you the signal. I want you to play it as though you really meant it, as befits a sad occasion.

SERGEANT And solemn, with your permission, sir.

GENERAL And solemn. Yes indeed. And solemn. All right, Bugler, on the double!

SERGEANT Lif right. Lif! Right!

GENERAL His Grace the Archbishop should be here at any moment. I am told his address to the nation will take about twenty minutes, which is a little longer than I had bargained for. It means we'll have to be right on our toes at the military end—otherwise it'll be a virtual certainty that the program will overlap into Children's Hour, which follows us at five sharp.

SERGEANT (*Shocked*) Good gracious me, sir, if I may make so bold—it's a bit shocking, isn't it? I mean, it's not as though we bury the Unknown Soldier every day, is it? I should have thought it'd do the nippers good to see the ceremony. After all, sir, they'll be doin' their military service soon enough . . .

GENERAL Oh certainly, Sergeant, I quite agree. The television boys have been most cooperative, and I'm sure, if the need arises, they'll let us run over.

(A disheveled man, the REBEL, *has entered, and is surreptitiously passing out pamphlets to the troop)*

SERGEANT Hullo—oh, it's you again, is it? Not content with four years in the fluting brig for desertion, you got to come here of all places with yer filthy coward-like ideas. Get out of it!

REBEL *(Laughing)* Still in good voice, Sergeant? That's what I like to hear. Care for a pamphlet?

SERGEANT Right! Any man takes a bit of paper from this stinking rebel's under arrest, got it?

GENERAL What seems to be the matter, Sergeant? Oh Lord, another troublemaker.

REBEL Another troublemaker? *The* troublemaker! Don't pretend you don't remember me. At Knossos, in the shadow of the blue hills, you had your first taste of me, didn't you? And you reacted as a soldier should. You ran me through . . . from the back. The last words I remember before I died—"Death is too good for this man!"

GENERAL The last words you remember before you died? Knossos? What the devil are you talking about?

REBEL You remember. You remember Knossos. The One Hundred and Eighteenth Legion.

GENERAL *(With a raucous yell—out of character)* AHHHH! Citizens of Rome, witness my triumph!

(Guiltily he passes his hand over his forehead)

REBEL (*In triumph*) You do remember!

SERGEANT (*Fuming*) Christmas, sir, let me get at 'im!

REBEL Christmas hadn't been thought of yet, but it was imminent. It was imminent.

GENERAL (*Sober, but decided*) Go away, before it's too late.

REBEL They tell me things have changed, Maximus Severus. They say this is a public park. There's even a rumor this is a free country.

SERGEANT (*Losing his head*) That's right. It's a free country. You're free to come 'ere, and I'm free to spread your guts on the lawn. (*The* REBEL *lies down*) What are you lying down for, you dung droppin'? Frightened, are you?

GENERAL Sar'nt!

REBEL Passive resistance.

SERGEANT Suits me. (*He begins kicking the motionless form of the* REBEL, *shouting*) It's a free country! I'll show you . . . how free it is . . .

GENERAL (*Not moving*) Sar'nt! Sar'nt!

(*A pretty little* WIFE *enters. She is in the last stages of pregnancy*)

WIFE Stop it!

(*The* SERGEANT, *who didn't stop for the* GENERAL, *stops for a woman*)

GENERAL Sergeant! You disobeyed an order!

SERGEANT (*Aghast*) I did? I can't think how it happened, sir. I was provocated. (*His sense of duty wins over his ability to find excuses. He stands stiffly*) Permission to put myself under arrest, sah!

GENERAL (*Absently*) I'll deal with you later. (*To the wife*) The public enclosure is over there, madam . . . that is, if you have a green ticket.

WIFE I don't need a ticket.

GENERAL I'm afraid you do.

WIFE I've a perfect right to be here. Whoever heard of a widow being kept away from her husband's funeral?

GENERAL I don't think you understand, madam. This is the funeral of the Unknown Soldier.

WIFE I know. That is the exact description of my husband.

GENERAL But this is the burial of no specific person, madam. It is a symbolic ceremony.

WIFE There's a body, isn't there? It must have been alive once.

GENERAL Of course, but it was selected because it was unrecognizable.

WIFE That's him! I knew it. He was never recognized by anyone—his face, his character, his personality—it was always the same.

GENERAL (*Tactful*) I sympathize with you in your great sorrow, naturally—but I feel bound to point out . . .

WIFE Oh, spare me your sympathy, man. I've no great sorrow. How the hell can you keep it up after all these centuries? No, I'm just bloody irritated by now. I've had enough of it. Dragging my feet under the weight of the child of an unknown father. Standing in line endlessly to claim my pension, filling in forms—and it wasn't always like that. But before—well, it was the poorhouse or the brothel . . .

REBEL Poor Virginia.

WIFE Virginia? Nobody's called me that for centuries!

REBEL It is your name, isn't it?

WIFE Not now it isn't . . . but I think it must have been once.

REBEL I thought so. I don't recognize your face, that's too much to expect . . . but I recognize your condition . . .

(A fierce gleam of sunshine suddenly breaks through the rain clouds. They all notice it. Seconds later, the ARCHBISHOP, *in full regalia, plunges onto the stage. He is also conscious of the change in the weather)*

ARCHBISHOP Ah! *(Touched by a minor grace)* I can't help but consider it significant that, at the very moment of my appearance at this scene of ennobling sorrow, a light from above should be shed upon us.

GENERAL Yes indeed, sir.

ARCHBISHOP *(Down to earth)* In any case, even if there's nothing in it, I believe it will benefit the television.

GENERAL Oh, undoubtedly, Your Grace.

ARCHBISHOP Twelve million is the latest figure, I hear.

GENERAL Twelve million?

ARCHBISHOP Twelve million viewers. The television experts estimate you will have the highest rating of the century, with the possible exception of the Olympic games.

GENERAL Well, I must say, Your Grace, that does tend to restore one's faith in certain values which . . .

ARCHBISHOP *(A little tartly)* I am making allusion to that in my address.

REBEL D'you remember a time before television was invented?

(The ARCHBISHOP *is mystified as to the whereabouts of the last speaker)*

GENERAL I must apologize, Your Grace.

ARCHBISHOP *(Spotting the* REBEL *on the ground)* Oh dear, another poor unfortunate who has suffered beyond his means in the recent war, no doubt. We must never lack the humility to minister to those who may possibly find comfort in our words. *(Adopting a gentle tone)* Yes, indeed I do remember a time before television was invented, my good man.

REBEL How did you communicate with your flock then?

ARCHBISHOP It was more difficult, but it was possible. It always has been possible, otherwise we wouldn't all be here today, as Christians. There was the radio.

REBEL And before that?

ARCHBISHOP The pulpit.

REBEL And before that?

ARCHBISHOP The marketplace.

REBEL And before that?

ARCHBISHOP The wayside shrine.

REBEL And before that?

ARCHBISHOP *(Puzzled)* Before that?

REBEL Before the Cross? Before the Scriptures?

ARCHBISHOP *(Gravely)* There was no before that for me . . . just darkness.

REBEL *(Rising)* Darkness? There was a fierce ray of sunlight then, after the rain, at Knossos. You gazed at the sky . . . at a black cloud with the silver sun edging its way behind it . . . when it shook itself free, blinding us, you rushed among us, shouting . . .

ARCHBISHOP *(With a great shout—out of character)* Victory is ours! Great is Mars, and we are his greatness! *(He grips his head as though in pain)* I do beg your pardon. I don't know what came over me . . .

GENERAL I know, Your Grace, the same thing happened to me just now—

WIFE *(Who has been staring at the* ARCHBISHOP. *Slowly)* Oh, now I remember you—every time it happened, there you were, right on time, with that sickly smile of consolation.

ARCHBISHOP *(A little taken aback. Icily)* Some widows have found the consolation I am able to offer, a fount of strength and wisdom.

WIFE How d'you know I'm a widow? I'm not even dressed as one.

ARCHBISHOP I thought you said . . .

WIFE I haven't opened my mouth since you arrived.

ARCHBISHOP Well, your presence here . . . I must have assumed . . .

WIFE I don't believe you. You remember, don't you?

REBEL Of course he remembers.

ARCHBISHOP Vaguely . . . I must admit . . .

GENERAL *(Uneasy)* Do be careful, Your Grace.

ARCHBISHOP Careful? Why?

GENERAL I sense a trap.

REBEL That's unusual for a military man.

SERGEANT *(Suddenly roaring)* What's that then! That man! What you got on your feet?

(They all direct their looks at the man at whom the SERGEANT *is pointing)*

14768 Boots, Sar'nt.

SERGEANT Call them boots? Look more like shiftin' sandals to me. Gold shiftin' sandals like bleedin' Cinderella!

35914 We've all got the same, Sar'nt. They look like boots to us.

GENERAL Regiment! Regiment, two paces forward march! *(The line of men advances two paces. They are seen to be wearing golden sandals)* Now look here, men . . . I know it's been a long war . . .

SERGEANT *(Beside himself)* Why argue with the chipped marbleheads? A swagger-stick round the vulnerables, that's what they're asking for!

GENERAL *(Aside)* Sergeant, I'll send you to the psychiatrist if you go on like this.

SERGEANT *(Quavering)* Oh no, sir, anything but that!

GENERAL You just can't talk like that any more in this day and age. Next thing, we'll have a strike on our hands.

71696 I can only say, sir, speakin' I believe for all the men, when we put them on this morning, they looked like boots to us.

(The men agree)

GENERAL And do they look like boots to you now?

14768 No, sir, but we was up half the night polishin' the ponderous things, the way the Sergeant likes them, so he can see his face in them in the mornin'.

REBEL Narcissus.

SERGEANT *(As though someone had called his name—out of character)* Yes? Did someone call me?

ARCHBISHOP Em . . . I neither wish to add to the present perplexities, General . . . nor do I wish to interfere with matters purely military . . . but in the interest of truth, I feel bound to draw your attention to your own footwear.

GENERAL Good heavens!

(The GENERAL*, too, is wearing golden sandals)*

WIFE Phew, it's hot . . . *(The* WIFE *takes her coat off and immediately loses her pregnancy. She wears a flimsy and seductive Roman tunic. The soldiers whistle)*

SERGEANT What's going on here? Sir! That woman! She's lost her child!

WIFE *(Hotly)* I never lost a child! I lost a husband, but I never lost a child! I'm a peasant. I've got a pride in my job. I just haven't started a child, that's all. I haven't met Julian yet.

SERGEANT *(Electrified)* Julian! That moon-struck molecule! I'll tie a lovers' knot wtih his arms and throw him in the Tiber if I ever lay my tentacles on him.

WIFE *(Violent)* I'll stuff your short-sword up your scabbard first!

GENERAL Sergeant! Pull yourself together! Tell the men to remove their gas-capes.

SERGEANT Sah! Stand by to remove gas-capes. Gas-ca-a-apes, re-move!

(The soldiers remove their gas-capes. They are dressed as Roman legionaries underneath. General surprise)

REBEL The crowd! It's vanished!

GENERAL *(Pale)* Vanished?

ARCHBISHOP The television cameras are still there!

REBEL Cameras? Those aren't cameras. Those are our regimental eagles, piled for the night.

(Sudden laughter from the soldiers while the REBEL *rips off his coat, to reveal the uniform of a legionary like the others)*

GENERAL *(On the verge of panic)* What are you all laughing at?

35914 The clothes you wear, Maximus Severus. You dress like a barbarian.

GENERAL A barbarian? *(Suddenly tremendous, changing in character in spite of himself)* I'm in command here! Put your uniforms on at once! We're on the television in half an hour! *(Nothing happens)* Sergeant, arrest them all!

SERGEANT *(Compassionate)* Your wits are frayed by the weight of your decision, Maximus Severus. Pray to the goddess of the night for rest free from phantoms.

GENERAL *(To the* ARCHBISHOP. *Hysterical)* Help us, Your Grace. Pray for sanity!

ARCHBISHOP *(Serious)* I have been asked to pray for prowess in war and wealth and potency, but never have I been asked to pray for sanity.

(He begins rocking with laughter, in which the men join. He takes off his mitre and throws it gaily into the air and out of sight)

GENERAL You too? Oh my God.

ARCHBISHOP *(Abruptly stern and menacing)* What was that? God—in the singular? Beware of thunderbolts, my poor misguided boy. Jove is indeed King of Olympus, father of the gods, but in flattering him it is unwise, most unwise, to ignore the others.

GENERAL *(Hardly audible)* The others?

ARCHBISHOP *(Nods sagely)* Let us pray. O Mighty Mars,

creator of widows, fount of tears, lend us your ear in your infinite mercilessness, and hear our prayer. Give us this day our daily victim, and teach us to kill without compassion, so that our civilizing mission may go unhindered by cries of mercy or the yells of the despoiled. Blind us to charity, and deafen us to entreaty, for ever, and ever. Amen.

(The GENERAL *rips off his cap. He wears a victor's laurels. He throws off his greatcoat. He is dressed as a Roman general)*

GENERAL *(All smiles)* Was that a good joke, men?

ALL *(In chorus)* A very good joke, Maximus Severus.

(He acknowledges their cheers like an untrustworthy modern wrestler. Quietly a young Roman wanders onto the stage)

SERGEANT *(Stern)* Where have you been, Julian?

THE UNKNOWN SOLDIER There are flowers in this valley which bloom late . . . little flowers we don't have in Italy . . . without much color, but with a strong and wholesome smell . . .

(He cups his hand to smell the flowers better)

GENERAL Which end of the valley?

THE UNKNOWN SOLDIER The far end, among the olive trees.

GENERAL Where the enemy lies encamped?

THE UNKNOWN SOLDIER *(Pleasant)* Yes. Exactly there. I talked to their sentries.

(A murmur of excitement)

GENERAL *(Holding up his hand for silence)* Dressed in your uniform?

THE UNKNOWN SOLDIER *(Smiling)* Oh yes, I haven't changed.

71696 Our Julian, a hero!

GENERAL In what language did you converse?

THE UNKNOWN SOLDIER In the language of signs. Men can always make themselves understood if they want to badly enough.

GENERAL (*Excited*) Well, man, out with it! What did you find out? Will they attack tomorrow?

THE UNKNOWN SOLDIER (*Laughing*) Oh no, I wouldn't have known how to frame such a question. And even if I could have done, I wouldn't have been able to make head or tail of the answer.

GENERAL (*Irritated*) Did you see nothing, at least?

THE UNKNOWN SOLDIER Oh yes. It's amazing the way the olive trees go almost into the sea down there. I've never seen olive trees grow so close to salt water.

GENERAL (*Frankly annoyed*) But the tents? The activity?

THE UNKNOWN SOLDIER Tents? Yes, I saw quite a few, but I didn't like to look too closely.

GENERAL Why on earth not?

THE UNKNOWN SOLDIER There were people inside them. They may have been undressing.

GENERAL (*Exploding*) Great gods! What did you talk about, then?

THE UNKNOWN SOLDIER About flowers.

GENERAL I don't believe it!

SERGEANT (*Taking over from the defeated* GENERAL) How many of them did you kill, Julian?

THE UNKNOWN SOLDIER Me? I didn't kill any. We found we had a common interest, you see.

SERGEANT Imperial Rome is at war, man! You know damn

well that it is your sacred duty to kill the other fellow before you have time to find out if you have a common interest or not!

GENERAL (*Taking over again, with terrible patience*) Julian, I'll give you one last chance to try and understand the meaning of military discipline. I do this only because it takes great physical courage to go up to a barbarian in the uniform of a Roman legionary the way you did.

THE UNKNOWN SOLDIER Why?

GENERAL The first lesson, Julian, is . . . never ask questions.

THE UNKNOWN SOLDIER How will I ever learn if I don't ask questions?

GENERAL There you are utterly and completely wrong. In order to obey orders, it is best to know nothing. To know everything is impossible, and to know something is merely confusing.

THE UNKNOWN SOLDIER Since you say it is impossible to know everything, and since you know more than me, it follows that you must know something.

GENERAL (*Tense*) You are losing your last chance, Julian. Stupidly. You are losing it stupidly. Your general tells you that field is red, soldier. What is your reply?

THE UNKNOWN SOLDIER Which field?

GENERAL (*Succumbing to his exasperation*) That field. Any field. They're all red!

THE UNKNOWN SOLDIER (*After a moment*) I suppose it is—sometimes—when the sun is setting.

GENERAL (*Roaring*) Not when the sun is setting. Now! Now!

THE UNKNOWN SOLDIER (*Rational*) No, sir, not now. Now the field is green.

SERGEANT (*Howling*) Idiot!

GENERAL (*After a moment*) Julian, watch this. Your general tells you that field is red. What color is that field?

ALL (*In chorus*) Red!

GENERAL Now do you understand?

THE UNKNOWN SOLDIER (*Contemplating the field*) It hasn't made it any redder, if that's what you mean, General.

GENERAL (*With a hopeless gesture*) Take him away, and kill him as an example.

THE UNKNOWN SOLDIER Since I'm the most stupid, General, who can I be an example to? They all think the field is red.

WIFE (*In a sudden outburst*) How can you say that field is red? That's blasphemy, you know, to change the color of Jove's green fields without permission.

(*The* GENERAL *hadn't thought of that. He looks uneasily at the* ARCHBISHOP)

ARCHBISHOP (*Ill at ease*) The pretty thing may be right. Jove's huge ear is everywhere. (*The stage grows darker*) See that black thunder cloud which has come between us and the sun? The weather is but the changing mood of the father of the gods.

GENERAL (*Calling to heaven*) Smile on us, Jove! I meant nothing by my words! The field is green! What color is the field, men.

ALL Green!

ARCHBISHOP See how the top left corner of the cloud suddenly turns down.

GENERAL Yes . . . Yes, I do . . . like the tongue of a dying bull.

ARCHBISHOP More like a down-turned thumb at some celestial games.

WIFE (*With trance-like authority*) Julian must not die!

(*They all glance at her, then back at the sky*)

ARCHBISHOP See, the thumb begins to turn up . . . and up . . . and up . . .

GENERAL (*Delighted*) Yes! Stay the execution!

ARCHBISHOP (*To the* WIFE) Who are you?

WIFE A girl from these parts.

ARCHBISHOP (*Tenderly*) How often the gods speak to us through the mouths of innocents! Now Julian will not die. He will just be whipped for insubordination as usual. Isn't that wonderful? Aren't you going to thank her, Julian?

THE UNKNOWN SOLDIER Thank you very much.

WIFE Why is he to be whipped?

GENERAL He failed to kill an enemy when he had a golden opportunity.

WIFE But there were more of them than him. If he'd killed one of them, the others would have killed him.

ARCHBISHOP (*With the patience of a nanny*) If they'd have killed him, there'd be no cause to whip him now, would there? I mean, you can't have it both ways.

WIFE I don't understand.

GENERAL (Amused) She's as bad as Julian.

ARCHBISHOP (*Equally amused*) Prettier, though.

GENERAL (*Calling out*) Whip Julian, and prepare for battle. We march within the hour!

SERGEANT About turn, lef', ri', lef', ri'—step smartly there!

ARCHBISHOP (*Detaining the* GENERAL) Oh, Maximus Severus, almighty Jove may well require a penance for your outrage. It would be best if you fought with your sword in your left hand.

GENERAL (*Amazed*) In my left hand? That's suicide! Where do you read your instructions?

ARCHBISHOP (*Testy*) Never mind. To each man his calling. (*There is an ominous roll of thunder. "I told you so"*) You stick to conquests, Maximus Severus, and leave the gods to me.

GENERAL (*Calling out*) I will fight with my sword in my left hand.

(*There is a flash of lightning*)

ARCHBISHOP The gods are gratified. (*The* GENERAL *exits. The* ARCHBISHOP *is alone with the* WIFE*—except for the* REBEL, *who lingers unseen*) Precious girl! Come, my little oracle, let me touch you . . .

WIFE No.

ARCHBISHOP Why not?

WIFE You frighten me.

ARCHBISHOP Perish the thought! I only wish to capture a particle of the divine grace which has passed through you.

WIFE It was common sense more than anything. (*Retreating*) How many strokes will they give Julian?

ARCHBISHOP (*Reasonable*) Five hundred.

WIFE (*Horrified*) Five hundred!

ARCHBISHOP Those are the regulations. But don't worry, my sweet child, there's not a man in the ranks who can count comfortably beyond fifty. Come now, gratify my craving. Let me touch you, my darling—my desire to do so springs from a purely religious urge.

REBEL It's amazing how many religious urges lie at the source of purely secular acts.

ARCHBISHOP Where have you sprung from, Dementius Praecox?

REBEL I have been loitering. An artist can always excuse his curiosity on the grounds of a search for material.

ARCHBISHOP Take no notice of him, my beauty. He's a poor fool of a sculptor they keep around to decorate triumphal arches at the end of minor campaigns.

REBEL Yes, my beauty, and if you examine the arches carefully, you will see the poor fool's comments on the mortal farce etched on the faces of the heroes.

ARCHBISHOP The subversive nature of your sculpture has not been lost on us. Why, it is impossible to tell your gods and your men apart. Even if you are an agnostic, at least remember that you are a Roman! The world looks to you for an example.

REBEL A Roman? Yes, alas. A despicable race. Garrulous, self-important, superstitious, hypocritical. There's so much still to learn, and what do we do? We teach.

ARCHBISHOP Great Jove! We tolerate you only because, up to now, the gods have tolerated you.

REBEL The gods tolerate me because they don't exist! Only man exists.

(There is a loud peal of thunder)

ARCHBISHOP *(Cringing)* Fool!

REBEL That was a peal of thunder, a natural phenomenon

with a purely scientific explanation. If, on the other hand, you persist in maintaining that almighty Jove aimed a thunderbolt at me, then, you must admit, he had the unusual experience of missing. (*He holds out his hand*) And so, my dear, don't be bamboozled by that old man. He is not an agent of the gods, but a man in priest's clothing. Be warned.

(*The* REBEL *exits*)

ARCHBISHOP Insufferable blasphemer! Come, my dear, you must be exorcised, in case his sacrilege has tainted the pristine loveliness of your soul. In the temple of Venus, your patron!

WIFE What do I have to do?

ARCHBISHOP Undress. Just slip off your tunic.

WIFE In front of you?

ARCHBISHOP Where else? The little demons have entered you by your ears. Together we will winkle the wicked little fellows out of all the orifices where they may be hiding.

WIFE (*Escaping*) You wish to find pleasure in me, not demons.

ARCHBISHOP In that it is a pleasure for a high priest to winkle out demons, that is quite true.

WIFE You wish to lie with me!

ARCHBISHOP Lie with you, stand with you, roll with you . . . the demons defy most positions. Come along now, you have nothing to fear from me. It is more an ecclesiastical formality than anything else.

WIFE Leave me alone!

(*She runs off*)

ARCHBISHOP Come back! Come here, in the name of all that's holy!

(He follows her, as THE UNKNOWN SOLDIER *staggers on. He is stripped to the waist and covered in blood. The* SERGEANT *helps him to walk)*

THE UNKNOWN SOLDIER You overdo everything you put your hands to.

SERGEANT *(With the gentleness of one who knows he has gone too far)* I lost count.

THE UNKNOWN SOLDIER You lost count more than once, and every time you started all over again from the beginning.

(He sinks to the ground)

SERGEANT Rest a while, Julian. I'll see to it that you're in the back row of the phalanx.

THE UNKNOWN SOLDIER That's what I don't understand about this army of ours . . . one moment you're like a bloodthirsty animal . . . next, you're all over me, like a childless aunt. And the others . . . they were happy to watch me being flogged . . . then they come gaping at my wounds, and offering to carry my spear into battle for me.

SERGEANT *(Squatting beside him, gentle and reasonable)* That's what's known as soldierly comradeship, Julian . . . I've been whipped more often than I care to remember . . . I wasn't always a sergeant, you know . . . no, came up through the ranks, I did . . . Would you care to see my scars?

THE UNKNOWN SOLDIER Not now, thank you.

SERGEANT Any time, any time, just ask. Came a time I

no longer minded the whip. Rather liked it, in fact. Proved to me I was a man.

THE UNKNOWN SOLDIER Don't you have any other proof? I mean . . .

SERGEANT (*Confidential and slow*) Civilians don't have our spirit, lad, because they're never cruel enough to one another to be surprised by one another's kindness.

THE UNKNOWN SOLDIER Yes, that's a point.

SERGEANT You want to think about that. Meanwhile, lie in the sun and let the blood congeal. You'll be a new man in about a month. Report to my tent in a quarter of an hour. I've got a little Ischian wine hidden in my pack. We'll share it.

(*The* SERGEANT *ruffles* THE UNKNOWN SOLDIER'S *hair affectionately, and goes. The* WIFE *runs on stage, her clothes in tatters, followed by the* ARCHBISHOP, *who seems on the verge of a heart attack*)

WIFE (*Falling on her knees*) Oh, Julian. What have they done to you?

THE UNKNOWN SOLDIER Why are your clothes torn?

ARCHBISHOP Because she's a disobedient country girl, who doesn't recognize friendship when she sees it . . . (*Glancing skyward*) Apollo has almost galloped into the free air again . . . I must prepare to give Victory her wings . . .

(*He walks slowly off, holding his heart*)

WIFE Your poor back . . . it would have been so easy to say the field was red.

THE UNKNOWN SOLDIER Easy? I don't think so. If I admit that, I'd be capable of admitting anything.

WIFE And can't you?

THE UNKNOWN SOLDIER Can you? They may flog you yet, for having run away from the high priest. Could you have given in to him?

WIFE No.

THE UNKNOWN SOLDIER How old are you?

WIFE Nineteen. And I have a Roman name. Virginia.

THE UNKNOWN SOLDIER Where do you live, Virginia?

WIFE I live on my uncle's farm, over there, on the hill. It's not much of a farm. One room for him, his family and the animals. I spend most of my time in my secret cave near the stream. Come with me. I'll show it you. I'll wash your wounds.

(He can hardly move, but does)

THE UNKNOWN SOLDIER What do you do in your cave?

WIFE I dream mostly.

THE UNKNOWN SOLDIER What else is there for the ignorant to do? We can't read—we can hear, but we can't always understand. But we can fly like birds into a world of color and of sound, which don't need explanation.

WIFE And meet above the clouds, where we can't make fools of ourselves.

THE UNKNOWN SOLDIER *(A sudden realization)* Perhaps that's why they punish me so often.

WIFE Why?

THE UNKNOWN SOLDIER I do all my dreaming during the day . . .

(They exit, walking at the pace of the invalid. There is a noise of marching men. The soldiers enter, the GENERAL *at their head. He carries his*

sword in his left hand. The SERGEANT *brings up the rear)*

SERGEANT Lef', ri', lef', halt!

GENERAL At ease, men. Where's Julian? Didn't you leave him here?

SERGEANT Yes, General, on this very spot.

GENERAL Didn't whip him too hard, did you?

SERGEANT What, me? We were laughing and joking about it! He must be able to move, mustn't he? Otherwise he'd still be here!

(The sun bursts out from behind the clouds blindingly. The ARCHBISHOP *rushes on. He carries a dead bird in one hand and a sling in the other)*

ARCHBISHOP Victory, victory, victory is ours! Great is Mars, and we are his greatness! Not only has golden Apollo shed his great light upon us, but I have killed a pigeon in flight, which, when I opened it, revealed itself to possess two livers! You all know what *that* means! A miracle!

(A great cheer goes up)

ALL *(In chorus)* Victory! Victory to Rome!

REBEL *(Entering)* You dropped this I believe, Your Lordship.

ARCHBISHOP What is it?

REBEL Another dead bird, Your Lordship, and very probably another miracle as well, for this one evidently was born with no liver at all.

ARCHBISHOP Where did you find it?

REBEL I followed you, Your Lordship, and it fell out of your robes.

ARCHBISHOP Give it here this instant! (*He seizes it in embarrassment*) You followed me where?

REBEL To the dovecote in the village, where you killed two domesticated doves and stuffed the liver of one into the other. Almighty Jove turned a blind eye.

ARCHBISHOP Listen to him, and the earth will open up and send us all headlong into the lower regions. I guarantee it!

(*There is an angry murmur among the men*)

GENERAL I will not stand for blasphemy, is that clear, not in the ranks, not before battle. Hey, sculptor, you of the remote passion and the delicate hands, come with us and see at first hand the heroism you so glibly depict on memorials.

REBEL I am dispensed of active duty as an official war artist.

GENERAL Seize him! You will be at the apex of our attack, unarmed!

REBEL (*With a wan smile*) And you will be just behind me, armed to the teeth. You know how to kill; perhaps I can teach you how to die. I am not afraid, because my statues will outlive the Empire.

(THE UNKNOWN SOLDIER *enters. The* WIFE *holds him by the hand*)

SERGEANT (*Rough*) Where have you been? Picking flowers again?

(*There is a ripple of laughter*)

GENERAL Join the line, Julian. With Dementius Praecox in the van.

THE UNKNOWN SOLDIER Narcissus told me I'd be near the back.

SERGEANT I never!

THE UNKNOWN SOLDIER You did! You even offered me some wine.

SERGEANT? Wine? Where would I get wine from?

GENERAL Wine? I've never heard you wish for wine before, Julian. (*Puzzled*) Are you afraid?

THE UNKNOWN SOLDIER Yes, very.

GENERAL What has made a coward out of you?

THE UNKNOWN SOLDIER The wish to live, I think.

GENERAL The wish to live?

(*Slowly he turns, and looks at the* WIFE)

WIFE When will you be back?

GENERAL Perhaps never. Why do you wish to know?

WIFE I am his wife.

(*Slowly a gale of laughter sweeps the stage, and all are affected except the* WIFE, THE UNKNOWN SOLDIER *and the* REBEL. *When the laughter threatens to die out,* 35914 *suddenly remembers, and repeats*)

35914 Where have you been? Picking flowers again?

(*The laughter surges again, but the* GENERAL *calls for order*)

GENERAL (*In good humor*) That's enough, men. We have enjoyed our laugh. Line up. Forward march. Let's have the song of the old whore of Pompeii.

(*Great acclaim greets this idea. As they go, they sing a marching song*)

94343 (*Singing*)

There was an old whore of Pompeii
Who had more than had her dayii.
To survive competition,
She got the permission
to charge only ten pence a layii.

ALL (*Singing*)

O—
A penny for this, a penny for that,
A penny each for a tit and tat,
A penny for what should have been fat
But was sadly shriveled and horribly flat.
O—
A penny for that, a penny for this,
A penny each for a hit and a miss,
A penny for what should have been bliss.
Hold your breath as you give her a kiss.

(*The* WIFE *follows them as they march, waving into the distance. The* ARCHBISHOP *just stands there, the dead birds in his hands. A subtle but perceptible change comes over him. The* WIFE *returns, and begins to exit*)

ARCHBISHOP (*Intimate and melancholy*) Virginia. I will not harm you. The fever's past.

WIFE Don't you march with them?

ARCHBISHOP No. I must prepare the triumph and rehearse the lamentations.

WIFE I'll leave you then.

ARCHBISHOP Not yet, please. It takes so much longer to understand one's actions than to perform them. I have killed two doves. Why? I only rarely look at birds when they are alive . . . they move about, and flutter . . . they're rather stupid, I suspect . . . I notice them out of the corner of my eye, and I never fear for their safety . . . they know how to save themselves much better than I know how to destroy them. Even if I kill them occasionally for food, I'm not really killing a bird . . . I'm killing a dish, a pie . . . in my mind, it's already steaming on a plate. But to kill these birds as I did, without reason, without honor, makes you notice your victim. (*He looks down at the birds*) Look at the miraculous network of feathers! The little bodies are growing cold in my hands. Their blue eyes are staring at me as though surprised that man, who has been throwing crumbs at them all their lives, should suddenly turn so treacherous. One of them has an olive branch in its beak. (*Deeply disturbed*) Tell me, Virginia, is it possible to love?

WIFE Is it possible not to love?

ARCHBISHOP I deserved such a cruel answer.

WIFE The months are passing as we stand here talking . . . and we always say the same words . . . and every time I tell you the truth, you always say I am cruel, and always ask for more . . . winter is here . . . can you feel it? And now it's almost spring . . . I feel unwell . . . I must get ready . . .

ARCHBISHOP So soon?

WIFE (*In pain*) I must get ready . . .

(*She goes, with difficulty. The* ARCHBISHOP *looks at the birds in silence*)

ARCHBISHOP I'd give the rest of my life if you could only fly away . . .

(*He kneels to bury them. From far away, out of tune, we can hear the song of the old whore of Pompeii. It grows in intensity, but seems in a minor key. The* GENERAL *leads his men on. He is intact, but the soldiers have lost legs, arms, hands, eyes, feet. Behind them are three prisoners in chains.* THE UNKNOWN SOLDIER *and the* REBEL *are missing. The* GENERAL *halts; The men likewise. The* GENERAL *raises his sword, of which only the hilt and an inch of blade remain*)

GENERAL Victory!

ARCHBISHOP (*Hollow*) The gods, in their infinite understanding, have blessed our arms.

GENERAL Bring forward the prisoners! Let the chronicle read that Maximus Severus, tamer of the Illyrians, scourge of the Bulgars, flagellator of the Avars, has won his most golden victory!

(*Very feeble cheer from the men*)

SERGEANT (*Grim*) Wait for it!

GENERAL (*Continuing*) His victory of victories, by putting to fight the . . . what is the same of your people again?

ENEMY LEADER The Oswingoths.

GENERAL Oswingoths? Are you sure?

ENEMY LEADER We are an Indo-European people with an Ugro-Finnish strain, the second cousins, as it were, of the Ostrogoths and the Visigoths, and like all small tribes, we were searching for a peaceful valley to settle in.

GENERAL You speak remarkably good Latin, if I may say so.

ENEMY LEADER (*Apologetic*) Very few people speak Oswingothic. We all know at least three languages, since we subsist on the mistrust of great peoples for one another. We live as go-betweens. We have to. We are weak in the arts of war.

GENERAL (*Flashing*) Weak? For the purposes of my triumph, you will be a tough, warlike race, and you, as its king, will have the honor of being dragged three times round the walls of Rome behind my chariot.

ENEMY LEADER That is extremely good of you, but isn't there some other way in which you can give expression to your vanity? Couldn't I, for instance, enter Rome comfortably in a cage?

GENERAL You fought bravely. You deserve the best.

ENEMY LEADER I'm quite agreeable to being thrown to the lions.

GENERAL The lions?

ENEMY LEADER We are such a poor people that we are naturally averse to waste. Even as you're being eaten by a lion, you have the pleasant feeling that you are at least providing some nourishment, whereas quite frankly to travel three times 'round the walls of Rome behind your chariot seems to me a waste of your time and my body.

GENERAL Are you trying to insult me?

ENEMY LEADER (*With a sigh*) I have the feeling that you are the kind of a person one succeeds in insulting far more often than one tries. At least be clement to my daughter.

GENERAL (*Smiling grimly*) I am too generous a man to be content with mere clemency. Enough! Take him away!

ENEMY LEADER Beware if we should ever meet again in freedom!

GENERAL You believe in reincarnation then?

ENEMY LEADER I have to. Our people could not live in honor on this earth without a fervent belief in a second chance. You don't need such a belief for the time being, because you are Roman.

GENERAL You admit our superiority!

ENEMY LEADER In force of arms, yes. In faith, no. You don't need it . . . yet . . .

(*The* GENERAL *drinks deeply from a flask, waving*

negligently with the other hand. The ENEMY LEADER *is taken away)*

ARCHBISHOP Where is Julian?

GENERAL Bring the next one forward! No, leave the woman till last! Who are you? Do you have the rank and quality to be dragged 'round Rome, or are you for the cage, the spittle and the urine?

INVENTOR *(Who speaks, surprisingly, with a thick German accent)* For neither, I think.

GENERAL *(Who shows early signs of an eventual inebriation)* There's presumption for you! What are you, then, to think yourself above degradation? A damned politician?

INVENTOR An inventor.

GENERAL *(Amused)* Inventor? What have you invented?

INVENTOR The stirrup.

GENERAL The what?

INVENTOR The stirrup. A rider puts his foot in the stirrup to guide the horse, and with the aid of spurs—another of my inventions—sharp pieces of metal worn on the heel —he can accelerate his horse while maintaining entire freedom of maneuver.

GENERAL *(Intrigued)* I noticed your invention at the height of the battle. Your leader could turn more rapidly than I could.

INVENTOR *(Categorical and aggressive)* The P.M.F. is increased tenfold under certain conditions.

GENERAL P.M.F.?

INVENTOR P.M.F. Power of Maneuver Factor.

GENERAL How would you like to work for Rome?

INVENTOR How much would I be paid?

GENERAL You are defeated! Dare you bargain with me?

INVENTOR I am never defeated while the stirrup lives! Without the stirrup, I give the Roman Empire twenty-five years—thirty maximum.

GENERAL But we have the stirrup now!

INVENTOR (*Tapping his head laconically*) You think I would be so foolish as to explain my invention to you if I didn't have something up here which will make even the stirrup look ridiculous?

GENERAL What is it?

INVENTOR How much will I be paid?

GENERAL You're not an Oswingoth, are you?

INVENTOR (*For a moment lachrymose and world-weary*) Oh, never mind where I come from . . . I had trouble at home . . . The Oswingoths did not pay well, but they gave me a hut of my own. (*His aggression reappears*) They treated me with respect . . . and I demand respect!

GENERAL A hundred talents a month.

INVENTOR Two hundred talents a week, with a laboratory of my own, and fifteen literate slaves.

GENERAL (*Staggered*) Fifteen slaves?

INVENTOR If they are Germanic, I can do with six; if they are Roman, at least fifteen.

GENERAL Do you dare . . .

INVENTOR Take it or leave it. Watch Rome go to defeat, or else give my genius the possibility of saving your decadent civilization a little longer.

GENERAL I will take you to Rome in chains. The Senate will decide.

INVENTOR (*Strident*) For every hour these chains are kept on, my price will go up by a talent a day!

GENERAL (*Shouting*) Take him to Rome without chains!

SERGEANT Lef', ri', lef', ri'.

INVENTOR (*Piercing*) I walk in my own rhythm!

(*The* SERGEANT *looks to the* GENERAL, *who shrugs his shoulders. They go out*)

GENERAL (*His good humor returning, he holds out his hand to the last captive, a strikingly handsome* WOMAN *dressed in furs. She comes forward slowly, impassively*) Here, Your Lordship, is the one captive which justifies the entire campaign. Come, my lovely . . . unlike her father, she will not be dragged round Rome in ignominy . . . she will enter my couch in triumph . . . naked except for my crown of laurels . . .

(*The* WOMAN *enters slowly, big with child*)

WIFE (*Eager*) Where is Julian?

(*The* GENERAL *looks at her, embarrassed. He gives the captive* WOMAN *his flask*)

GENERAL Drink!

(*She does so, obediently*)

ARCHBISHOP (*Quietly*) Go your way, Virginia. I am not fit to console you.

WIFE (*Slowly*) He's dead?

(*The* GENERAL *reclaims his flask*)

GENERAL (*Sincere after his fashion*) For a soldier, death matters less than the manner of dying. Rest assured, widow, he died like a Roman.

ARCHBISHOP Foolishly.

GENERAL Before the enemy was even in sight, I had drawn my sword to stab the sculptor in the back, the coward's death befitting the crime of sacrilege, when, by some instinct, Julian turned and threw himself before the blade . . . it was too late . . . I impaled them both. There was no time to bury them . . . and (*He laughs*) there was no one left to fashion a tombstone . . . they lie together, the traitor and the fool, like lovers, under the open sky. (*In an epic manner*) When they are found, nothing will be known about the treachery of one, or the folly of the other . . . men will say to themselves, Rome passed this way in all her indestructible majesty, leaving two unknown sons as viceroys in death.

(*He is moved by his own eloquence*)

WIFE (*Moving slowly in the direction of the battle. Numb*) How far away are they?

GENERAL (*Outraged*) Do you not dignify your sorrow by shedding tears? Look, I am weeping.

WIFE (*Beyond tears*) Give me time . . . give me time . . . tears are private things . . . I will find them . . .

(*She exits*)

GENERAL There's your average foreigner for you. Any Roman matron would be wailing and beating her breast! She has done her best to ruin my evening . . . I've never seen anything less considerate. (*To the* WOMAN) Come to my tent. I will find solace in your arms . . .

ARCHBISHOP (*Wringing his hands*) Oh, my son, my son.

GENERAL (*Annoyed*) Why do you call me "my son"? I am not your son.

ARCHBISHOP What did I call you? My son? I don't know why I did that. I feel I am sickening for some condition more terrible and more wonderful than death.

GENERAL What's the matter with you?

ARCHBISHOP I tried to pray to Jove, but my heart's not in it. I am no longer blinded by his great light—I see only effigies in my mind, accumulating dust. Jove is inadequate.

GENERAL (*His arm around the* WOMAN. *Laughing*) If it's hallucinations you're after, get drunk.

ARCHBISHOP Kill me, Maximus Severus.

GENERAL What? (*Laughs again*) Why die for a cause you no longer believe in?

ARCHBISHOP I no longer believe in Rome.

GENERAL (*Harsh*) Then pretend, as we all do on occasion!

ARCHBISHOP I no longer can.

GENERAL What? You do it better than any of us. A pigeon with two livers indeed! And it's a miracle that I'm still alive fighting with my sword in my left hand.

ARCHBISHOP If you felt there was no religious reason for the penance I imposed, why did you do it?

GENERAL (*Eager to leave*) For the sake of the men! Only leaders like you and me can afford the luxury of believing in nothing but themselves. It is the men who must believe in the panoply of gods. Without this fiction of divinity, Rome would be powerless. Great gods, Your Lordship, a great general must be able to make mistakes, huge mistakes, tragic mistakes, without disillusioning the soldiery. There's only one way of doing it—and that is by creating omnipotent and capricious gods, in whose hands we are but playthings. But you know this as well as I do. Our interests coincide. They always have done. Are you listening?

(*The* GENERAL, *who is on his way out with his captive, is forced to stop by the surprising intensity of the* ARCHBISHOP'S *manner*)

ARCHBISHOP I hear another voice, dim, distant, as yet indistinct, like a small child crying in my heart.

GENERAL You are becoming a woman, perhaps?

ARCHBISHOP Make jokes at your peril! The voice is there, Maximus Severus, and it will take over my temple, because it is alive. It is the voice of love.

GENERAL Voice of love? (*Impatient*) All right. You can have the girl after I've done with her.

ARCHBISHOP I am unworthy to touch this sweet woman. My hands would soil her.

GENERAL What are you talking about? She's a mere barbarian.

ARCHBISHOP A mere barbarian . . . Maximus, my son, before it is too late, set her free. Speak to her with the charm and tact of which you are sometimes capable. Take her to your tent, but as your guest. Do not outrage her.

GENERAL Idiot! What's her body for?

ARCHBISHOP To tempt you . . . and to be respected.

GENERAL Are you ill?

ARCHBISHOP I am cured. (*He smiles*) I no longer have to believe. I know. I am at peace. I will plant seeds in your mind which will blossom into a harvest, and long after I have gone, I will still be with you.

GENERAL (*To the* WOMAN) Come.

ARCHBISHOP (*With great gentleness*) Are you afraid of me now?

GENERAL Afraid?

ARCHBISHOP Do you suddenly sense my strength?

GENERAL You're mad.

ARCHBISHOP Your pleasure will be cold, your face expressionless, as that of a copulating dog—for that is what you have made of yourself.

GENERAL (*Furious*) Enough! (*He places his hand on the hilt of his sword*) You asked for death a while ago! I am known for my generosity.

ARCHBISHOP Seek for a mirror to your pleasure in her eyes —all you find there is patience. She will lie under the weight of your coarseness, thinking other thoughts, waiting for the puppy to have done with its petty ecstasies.

GENERAL (*Drawing his sword*) It won't take much to put an end to your voice.

ARCHBISHOP (*As sweet as ever*) And when you fall into your ugly warrior's sleep, she will look at you with pity —is this little fornicator the emblem of mighty Rome? Is the strength of the eagle in its loins alone?

GENERAL Aah!

(*He runs the* ARCHBISHOP *through with his sword*)

ARCHBISHOP (*Falling to his knees with an echo of the* GENERAL'S *shout*) Aaah! . . . Thank you, Maximus . . .

GENERAL (*Aghast*) What have you made me do?

ARCHBISHOP I have taught you remorse . . . I have given you a conscience as a parting gift . . .

GENERAL Why did you make me kill you?

ARCHBISHOP Because you are weak, my son. There's no weakness more pernicious than the weakness of the strong.

GENERAL (*Examining the* ARCHBISHOP *as though he were some curious, half-dangerous animal*) Why are you smiling?

ARCHBISHOP (*Begins to laugh very softly, and shakes his head feebly*) What a question . . .

GENERAL (*Slow*) Do you derive pleasure from suffering? (*No reply. The* GENERAL *loses his temper. He stabs the* ARCHBISHOP *again and again*) There! There! Enjoy yourself! (*The* ARCHBISHOP *rolls over and dies. The* GENERAL *stands there for a moment, panting. He returns his sword to its scabbard*) Go to my tent. (*The* WOMAN *begins to go*) Say something.

WOMAN Yes.

GENERAL Say something else. Tell me I am mad.

WOMAN I can't.

GENERAL Why not?

WOMAN I am your slave.

GENERAL I despise myself. Do you despise me?

WOMAN No.

GENERAL (*Tired*) You can't give me satisfaction. Go to my tent.

WOMAN Yes, Maximus.

(*She exits*)

GENERAL I will sleep in the grass . . .

(*He goes out in the opposite direction. It grows lighter. The men gather, severally, as though for an imminent parade. 14768 is the type of hedgehog-browed individual with a curved muscular neck who is usually the runner-up in unit boxing competitions. 35914 is the joker of the unit, optimistic to the point of abnormality. 71696 has quite unnecessary dignity and some sickening middle-class virtues. He is redolent of the quartermaster's stores. 94343 affects whatever appearance happens to be in vogue, since there is safety in conformity. They still bear their wounds*)

35914 What time's parade, lads?

94343 Usual time. There's nothing posted to the contrary.

71696 By rights we should have a day off. How long's it been, six years?

35914 I've lost count.

14768 By rights, once we're talkin' about the letter of the law, we should get ten days off—that's if they don't skimp the old man on his triumph.

71696 I wouldn't put it past them—to skimp him on his triumph.

14768 Nor would I. Wouldn't put it past them.

94343 (*Anxious*) Not past them, I wouldn't put it.
(*They all pause*)

71696 (*To* 35914) What's up with you? Look as though you'd gapin' seen a ghost.

35914 It's worse. Look!
(*The* SERGEANT *enters in medieval costume—green tights, crimson jerkin with a coat of arms on it, upturned shoes of immense length, and a rakish cap with an immense feather. The men try to contain their laughter*)

SERGEANT (*Forestalling their laughter with a rising cadence of admonition, he loses his temper*) You mucous-snotted, ordure-replete set of half-hatched sparrow chicks!

35914 What's that? The new uniform, Narcissus?

SERGEANT What's that you called me? Some insult?

35914 (*Puzzled*) That was your name when last we saw you.

SERGEANT And when was that?

14768 A few minutes ago . . . after the battle. You remember.

71696 Ah no, I give it longer than that. Close on an hour, I give it.

94343 It may have been yesterday . . .

14768 (*Violent*) You'll be sayin' it was last week next!

94343 (*With a sense of the occult*) Time's a funny thing, you know. I'll be on the safe side. I'll say it was a month ago.

35914 Once you say it's a month, it might as well be a year . . . or a century.

SERGEANT Now you're getting warmer. I'll overlook your tunics this once, you're all too gloomy ignorant to know better, but if you go on standin' on one leg much longer, and hiding your arms and hands behind your backs, and winkin' at me, I'll really start showin' you who's the freed-man and who are the fiefs.

71696 We was wounded.

SERGEANT What? Them little scratches? Call them wounds? (*Sarcastic*) Haven't they healed yet, after all this time? Tut-tut. What d'you want me to do? Kiss 'em better? (*Mysteriously their arms, legs and eyes reappear. They stretch their rediscovered limbs as though they have stiffened with inaction*) That's more like it. Now move! Move! Move! (*They run and stumble off, frightened. The* SERGEANT *spots the figure of the dead* ARCHBISHOP) What's this, then? Another of you idle malingerers playin' dead? (*He kicks the* ARCHBISHOP, *who sits up with a start*) Oh, Father Benedict! Beg pardon!

ARCHBISHOP (*Suffering*) Oh, Odbert, what a dream! A beautiful pagan in a bearskin, it was . . . Every time she parted her lips to embrace me, a flight of doves fell out of her mouth, and dropped dead at my feet. I gathered their corpses in my arms until I could no longer stand under their weight.

SERGEANT That must have been when you fell down, my Lord Abbot.

ARCHBISHOP (*Whose speech is slurred*) Quite right. Then I remember rejecting them, and gathering the pagan to me. I could feel her warm, firm breasts and the richness of her thighs, and just as I was preparing to enjoy her, a Roman came along and stabbed me in the side for no reason at all.

SERGEANT That must have been my foot, Lord Abbot.

ARCHBISHOP Ah yes. You saved me from the devil, Odbert.

SERGEANT Glad to have been of service to you, sir.

ARCHBISHOP Oh, my head. The fact is, I don't drink.

SERGEANT I know that, Father Benedict.

ARCHBISHOP I am merely on the trail of the damnedest after-dinner cordial . . . a couple more herbs and I'll have it, Odbert, and perhaps one day, it will bear my name.

SERGEANT I dare say, Father Benedict.

ARCHBISHOP Yes, Odbert . . . and not only will it give pleasure, but it will ensure the solvency of the monasteries in times of little faith. (*He tries to rise, but cannot, even with the* SERGEANT*'s help. Heartfelt—on his knees*) We live in godless times, my friend.

SERGEANT (*Grim*) Indeed we do, my Lord Friar.

ARCHBISHOP How is the cathedral coming?

SERGEANT Slowly, my Lord Friar, but I like to think, surely.

ARCHBISHOP We must finish it soon. Cathedrals are shooting up all over Europe. A city is judged by the height of its spire and the length of its nave. Already I am beginning to think ours is a little on the small side.

SERGEANT We've no shortage of labor, Father Benedict. We can afford to make mistakes.

ARCHBISHOP (*With fearful sincerity, tugging at the* SERGEANT'*s sleeve*) Odbert, our arches must be more Gothic, our gargoyles more harrowing, our glass more stained than any of our rivals'. There is a faith-race on, my friend, which we cannot afford to lose.

SERGEANT (*Lifting him up, and helping him to walk*) I'll see to it, Lord Abbot. I'll have the men on cathedral fatigues twenty-four hours of the day. We won't be found wanting where faith is concerned.

(*As they go, the* GENERAL *appears from behind an obstacle. He has been listening. He is now a medieval count, a pampered, petulant exquisite in his coal-black wig. He watches them go with manifest displeasure—then hears a noise. His expression changes to one of indecent eagerness. He hides again.* THE UNKNOWN SOLDIER *wanders on, arm in arm with his bride, the* WIFE, *who is heavily pregnant*)

THE UNKNOWN SOLDIER (*Reciting*)
O, I sometimes think my heart will burst its banks,
Sweet girl, and that this fragile frame cannot contain
Such trumpeting delights forever. Even in idleness,
While carving your name upon some crusty bark, you
Invade the corner of my eye, and fill my mind
With your dear presence as surely as when we're locked
In love. I cut my thumb, for in all work,
You are my lovely negligence.

WIFE (*Reciting*)
Not always was it so. For wert thou negligent, dear boy,
My belly would not now swell with unknown fruit
And cause me to waddle like an ailing duck
While my *mind* is pregnant with images of grace.

THE UNKNOWN SOLDIER
And we can laugh as well! What a shower of miracles . . .

WIFE
A shower? Take refuge then.

THE UNKNOWN SOLDIER (*Falling to his knees before her*)
Not I! Bare-headed
I kneel beneath them, my eyes uplifted, my mouth op'd wide
To drink in pleasures while those pleasures last.

WIFE (*Sadly*)
Ay, there's the truth, for nothing lasts.

THE UNKNOWN SOLDIER
Nothing lasts
But memory and hope.

WIFE
And memories of hope.

THE UNKNOWN SOLDIER
And hope of memories when we are old.
My love for thee encompasses all seasons in a second,
Stretches beyond the confines of mortality, baffles time,
Cheats age, and scoffs at Providence itself . . .
Have I not known thee for a thousand years, and more?
Yet could I love thee then as I love thee now?
Has it not taken a luxury of time, to know
What now we know?

WIFE
To feel what now we feel?
When first we met, it was the brief love

The moth feels for the flame. A mere winking of an eye
And all was over. We had lived, and loved.
You had even died. But I could never guess then
What I had lost.

THE UNKNOWN SOLDIER

Lost but found again.
For what is love but endless rediscovery?
To see thee once is to see thee for all time
And to see thee not at all. A thousandth look
Is but a confirmation of the first, and yet is different.

WIFE

I know only this, in all simplicity. I am a book
Thou hast chosen from the vast library of women.
Open me. I lie open. The wind may lose my place,
But not another reader. I, like all volumes, have secrets
To be read between the lines, but the words are these as well.
Unread, I am not worth the binding.
Unfinished, I am not worth beginning.
Read, I surrender what rewards I may.
Understood, I am a life's companion.
Rewritten, I may yet be improved upon.
Lent to an illiterate, I go to waste.
I cannot bring myself to life. Only he who reads me well
Will know what is written there, and, knowing what is written,
Will know also that which destiny has failed to write.
But be not hard. Judge me not always by perfection's rote.
Think, instead, and humbly, how wonderful it is
The pages are not blank. One final word:
Read not with impatience, for though life, they say, is short,
At moments it seems long, and time will turn my pages
Soon enough . . .

Howard DaSilva as the ARCHBISHOP.

THE UNKNOWN SOLDIER

My eyes are weary from so much study.
Let me put you by, then, to read again
The early chapters at some later hour. I close the book.
And seal my pleasure with a kiss . . .

(*They kiss with increasing fervor. The* GENERAL *looks out of his hiding place*)

GENERAL (*Aside, reciting*)
How? How's this? The ignorant know bliss
While I, in my noble loneliness, do search for fancies,
To cajole my sad and complicated mind—
The colloquy of poets, the plucking of a casual string,
The ponderous baggage of Westphalian philosophers,
The simple songs of peasants, even those degrading practices—
Love of wayward women and of fearful boys—
The wild excesses of the chase, love's substitute—
All are mobilized to satisfy my spirit's hunger,
To slake my parched soul's dismal thirst.

(*The lovers break. They see the* GENERAL)

THE UNKNOWN SOLDIER
Most Noble Count!

GENERAL

Kiss on, youth! And may the soft breeze
Waft a few particles of revivifying pollen
Upon this dying plant. You spoke to each other in verse.
Why?

THE UNKNOWN SOLDIER I was speaking normally, sir.

GENERAL Normally? Lass, could you speak to me as you spoke to this youth?

WIFE No.

GENERAL Try. (*The* GENERAL *prepares to listen, taking up*

a romantic stance. The WIFE *and* THE UNKNOWN SOLDIER *look at each other in embarrassment)* No?

WIFE No. I'm truly sorry, sir, I can't.

GENERAL *(Suspicious)* You hadn't learned it by heart, had you, from some learned volume—stolen from my library?

THE UNKNOWN SOLDIER We can't read, sir.

GENERAL Why, then, did you compare yourself to a book?

WIFE It was a . . . a manner of speaking, sir.

GENERAL It was a manner of singing. You can't remember any of it, can you?

THE UNKNOWN SOLDIER *(After a look at the* WIFE*)* No, sir.

GENERAL You mean all that is lost?

WIFE It comes out differently, sir, every time we see one another.

GENERAL If you are left alone, is that it? In other words, I'm not wanted—not wanted in my own sixty thousand acres! *(His eyes half-closed)* I seem to remember you from some other field . . . a field which sprouted rosemary and thyme . . . you came forward with that same irritating look of impervious innocence, a bunch of ridiculous little flowers gathered in your fist . . .

THE UNKNOWN SOLDIER I have often gathered flowers, sir.

GENERAL *(Slow—his eyes half-shut in reminiscence)* And you . . . that swollen womb is nothing new . . . that look of health, that indecent sparkle . . . that galling smell of the open air and of clean linen . . . you asked a question . . .

WIFE This will be our first child, sir.

GENERAL Curious . . .

(The SERGEANT *marches on with his men. They carry bows and arrows)*

SERGEANT Lef', ri', Lef', ri', halt! Three hearty cheers for the Count of Rochentière. Hip hip . . .

ALL *(In chorus)* 'Ray!

SERGEANT You can do better than that! Hip hip . . .

ALL 'Ray!

GENERAL *(A languorous falconer's hand aloft)* I am touched by your loyalty. Where are you going?

SERGEANT To the archery range, may it please you, to test the Professor's new weapon.

GENERAL Good. Good. Test it well, for it is fiendish.

SERGEANT *(Spotting* THE UNKNOWN SOLDIER*)* What are you doing there then? *(A murmur among the men)* Where you been?

THE UNKNOWN SOLDIER Dead, I believe.

SERGEANT Fall in then!

GENERAL Do not be hard on him, Odbert. The lad's a poet.

SERGEANT A what? Yes, sir. Very good, sir.

(The INVENTOR *enters, wearing the macabre black cap of medieval men of learning, and metal-rimmed glasses. He carries a device looking like a crossbow, but seemingly twice as heavy. He has difficulty in transporting it)*

INVENTOR *(As German as ever)* I thought you were going to send some men to fetch the weapon! I am engaged here as a man of learning, not as a manual laborer!

SERGEANT Beg pardon, Professor. You, the poet, take the weapon, and fall in!

(THP UNKNOWN SOLDIER *takes the weapon. He falls momentarily to his knees*)

THE UNKNOWN SOLDIER Ooh! It's heavy!

INVENTOR (*Rasping*) It is not heavy! It is an infantry weapon, therefore it is light!

SERGEANT Lef', ri', lef', ri' . . .

(*The men, including* THE UNKNOWN SOLDIER, *march off*)

INVENTOR (*Beaming*) With my new weapon, Count, you will soon be master of the known world!

GENERAL I am gratified, Professor . . . but how to conquer the unknown world?

INVENTOR (*Irritated, after a momentary hesitation*) One thing at a time please.

(*He exits. The* GENERAL *turns to seek the* WIFE)

GENERAL Now that we are alone, my dear . . .

(*He fails to find her. The* ARCHBISHOP *re-enters behind him*)

ARCHBISHOP Ah, there you are, my son. I have been waiting for you in the chapel. Will you not confess today?

GENERAL I do not feel like confessing today, Father, I have too much on my mind.

ARCHBISHOP My son, you must. I cannot allow you to squander your fortune on pardons when there is an easier, cheaper way.

GENERAL Does the money for the pardons ever get halfway to Rome?

ARCHBISHOP Ten Hail Mary's for that crack, my son. Kneel with me here, if you will. I will draw my cowl over my head to preserve the necessary anonymity. I have things to tell you.

(They kneel)

GENERAL You have things to tell me?

ARCHBISHOP I must confess you first.

GENERAL My mind is troubled, Lord Abbot. I have had women—enjoyed them in the vulgar parlance—yet I did not enjoy them. They come to make my bed—anonymous women, their arms full of sheets. They are my serfs. I exercise my rights. All passes joylessly, in silence.

ARCHBISHOP All this since yesterday?

GENERAL Since this afternoon, I believe. Lads too—they make a change.

ARCHBISHOP Heavens! Is there no end to your appetites?

GENERAL I have found no vice which appeases me for longer than the time it takes to perform it.

ARCHBISHOP My son, there is no alternative to the hair shirt and the scourge.

GENERAL The hair shirt is bad for the skin.

ARCHBISHOP Better the skin should suffer than the soul.

GENERAL Men only see the skin.

ARCHBISHOP Our Father sees them both. Come, my son, I will thrash you lightly.

GENERAL I have not finished my confession.

ARCHBISHOP Is there more then? Is it possible?

GENERAL My waking hours drift into night—my sleeping hours, if I ever sleep, drift into day. I sometimes wake the cooks at night to banquet all alone—and I sometimes retire at noon. I may walk in sleep or lie abed awake—

where dreams begin and actions end I am not sure. I wonder, therefore, if I perform these horrid deeds at all, or whether they are not all done in my head, for my solitary delight.

ARCHBISHOP Are you sure of this?

GENERAL I can be sure of nothing now.

ARCHBISHOP Men of high station deserve the benefit of our doubt. Since you are half-drowned in dreams, my son—I command you to dream that you have been soundly whipped by me. (*The* GENERAL *writhes and howls as though he is being flogged*) Not now, my son. Your fustigation can wait. You have given me an earnest of your intention to relish every blow, and that is enough to go on with. I need to talk to you.

GENERAL What is it?

ARCHBISHOP You need a change of air, my son. Your skin is flaky, your complexion sallow, while your mind festers with depravity.

GENERAL What do you suggest?

ARCHBISHOP I have no suggestion; Rome has.

GENERAL Rome?

ARCHBISHOP His Holiness himself! On his behalf I can promise you, in writing—listen carefully—a remission of all sins, past, present and *future*. You realize what this means? A passport to paradise!

GENERAL (*Dry*) What are his conditions?

ARCHBISHOP Why do you speak so quickly of conditions?

GENERAL Because I am a man, and so is His Holiness. Why are you so disappointed?

ARCHBISHOP I expected at least a moment of unmitigated delight.

GENERAL I will express delight when and if I feel it. What are his conditions?

ARCHBISHOP Take a crusade to the Holy Land, my son.

GENERAL A crusade? You call that a change of air? Mosquitoes, pestilence and sores?

ARCHBISHOP All *future* sins?

GENERAL A crusade may last for years! Armand de Queslin and Raymond de la Baule never came back at all!

ARCHBISHOP They are in heaven at this moment, and better off than here. I guarantee it!

GENERAL I may miss ten, fifteen hunting seasons.

ARCHBISHOP Copulation to your heart's desire, free of moral charge.

GENERAL No more chamber music!

ARCHBISHOP The music of gold cascading into coffers.

GENERAL No.

ARCHBISHOP (*An appeal to reason*) My son, Christianity needs you.

GENERAL (*Slowly*) And before it was Imperial Rome, wasn't it?

ARCHBISHOP (*Slowly*) You remember, do you?

GENERAL Oh yes . . . memory comes fitfully, in flashes . . . I remember then being a victim of your faith. You made me stab you, and after that I knew no peace. I had killed an unarmed man at his own request. Can one go further in servility? No, I will not go to the Holy Land.

ARCHBISHOP Can't you see that you have had your revenge already, my son? His Holiness, in his infinite understanding, offers you a pardon for sins as yet uncommitted, and yet you say, with reprehensible arrogance, that he is only a man. If he is a man, how much less of a man am I, and what is my pardon worth? I can no longer absolve you. You cheat at every confession.

GENERAL You came here as my confessor, with endorsed credentials!

ARCHBISHOP But since then you have worn away my faith as surely as water wears away a rock. You have had your revenge, my son. I came to lift you off the ground; you have brought me to my knees. I will not exonerate you before God. You are on your own.

GENERAL (*Slowly*) Religion is blackmail. It holds a man's opinion of himself to ransom.

ARCHBISHOP It assesses the value of a man's opinion to himself.

GENERAL Religion is superstition. It makes a man conscious of the alternatives.

ARCHBISHOP Religion is the work of God . . .

GENERAL Perfected by the devil. I will go to Jerusalem.

ARCHBISHOP Deo gratias! (*Chanting*)

Alleluia . . . Alleluia . . .
We go to the land of our Lord
To clash with the infidel horde.
And if we should die,
To heaven we'd fly—
Father Benedict gave us his word.
Alleluia . . . Alleluia . . .

(*The men file in, carrying crossbows and religious symbols. They chant with the* ARCHBISHOP. *He leads them in a procession. He goes off majestically with the court, while the men go round in diminishing circles, the song growing feebler as the sun now beats fiercely on them. They fall exhausted, one by one*)

SERGEANT (*Comatose, once they have fallen*) Right. Fall out! Wait . . . for . . . it! Fall not!

(*He falls to the ground*)

35914 (*Feeble*) You've got some water, by the holy cross! Why can't we have a sip?

SERGEANT (*Feeble*) It's holy water, for the daily benedictions. You lumber-headed blunderbumpkins won't never be able to tell the secular water from the divine, will you?

94343 We seen you take a swig.

SERGEANT I was testin' its freshness, got it? In *case* we're reduced to using it. I never ask the men to do nothing I'm unwilling to do myself.

35914 How was it then?

SERGEANT Un-ruddy-drinkable. Satisfied?

THE UNKNOWN SOLDIER No, I'm not satisfied . . .

SERGEANT Eh?

THE UNKNOWN SOLDIER They didn't even give me time to say good-bye.

SERGEANT When you get back, my boy, there'll be a large bouncin' lad to greet you. That'll be a nice surprise, won't it?

REBEL A large bouncing lad about twenty-five years old, the way this campaign's going.

SERGEANT I don't want no rumination from you. I got my eye on you. If it wasn't so flamin' hot, I'd settle you.

REBEL Well, it is so flaming hot. You can't even see to keep your eye on me. Every time you blink, the perspiration rolls in.

THE UNKNOWN SOLDIER Death is a waste of time. (*They all stir, despite their stupor*) All men die at night, and it holds no fear when it goes by the name of sleep. What holds fear is dying.

(*The* WIFE *appears*)

WIFE Why do you speak of death? Have you forgotten . . .

THE UNKNOWN SOLDIER I have remembered. To die is but search for you again.

SERGEANT (*Gruff*) Who are you talkin' to?

THE UNKNOWN SOLDIER What would you write to me, I wonder, if you could write?

WIFE I am not lonely, because I am alone. The men have gone. The hunting horns are silent. There is no mischief anywhere. Even the beasts of the forest wander into the pasture unafraid. There's nothing to confess. And what would you write?

THE UNKNOWN SOLDIER

I'd write, I'd write . . . let me see . . .
I'd write that I am lonely because I am not alone.
My loneliness travels with me. Six thousand men carry it
And I carry theirs for them. I share my secrets
As I share my water and my food.

WIFE But why? These men were never friends of yours.

THE UNKNOWN SOLDIER Where there is no choice, all men are friends. (*Pause*) Why are you silent?

WIFE

I feel another journey coming.
The child begins to stir, and I know my cue for tears.
I will not cry. I will not cry at all. Now or then.

ARCHBISHOP (*Entering*) Why are you crying, my child?

WIFE (*Angry, turning her head away*) Crying? I am so angry with my man!

ARCHBISHOP Angry, child? Can he help his absence any more than I can help my presence?

WIFE Why are you here to bother me?

ARCHBISHOP They deemed I was too old to die before my time. Rest assured, your man will return . . .

THE UNKNOWN SOLDIER I have marked my place in the book. Even if it drops from my hand, I will know every detail of what went before.

WIFE Why should you die?

THE UNKNOWN SOLDIER A coward can survive. He finds out nothing. He merely stays alive.

WIFE Is that not enough?

THE UNKNOWN SOLDIER No.

SERGEANT (*Crawling over to* THE UNKNOWN SOLDIER) Here, take a sip of water, man. You're ravin'!

THE UNKNOWN SOLDIER I don't want it.

SERGEANT (*As violent as he can manage*) Take it! That's an order! You're under-bloody-mining us all!

(*Calls of "Take it," "Go on," etc., are heard. The* GENERAL *enters in full armor, hardly able to move*)

GENERAL Water, for the love of God!

SERGEANT Platoon! To your feet!

(*They struggle to their knees*)

GENERAL Forget the protocol! Just give me water.

SERGEANT It is blessed.

GENERAL I don't care if it's perspiration of a saint, I must have it!

SERGEANT (*As he gives the* GENERAL *his flask*) It's the last we have.

(*The* GENERAL *drains it*)

GENERAL Is there no more? (*The men look at each other, dismay and hatred suddenly written on their faces. A weird sound is heard)* The infidel! Every time I put this armor on, I feel a pressing need to relieve myself.

SERGEANT We can get you out of there in half an hour.

GENERAL With the enemy so close? Are you mad? No, no, it must be a nervous reaction to the imminence of battle. It will pass. Where did the sound of the trumpet come from?

SERGEANT *(Pointing right)* From over there.

ALL *(Pointing in all directions but one)* There, there, there.

GENERAL Then we will advance in the opposite direction. With a little luck we may outflank them.

SERGEANT Form up! Shoulder crossbows! *(The men form up with the greatest difficulty)* Any order of the day, sir?

GENERAL Instruct every man to pray for my safety.

SERGEANT You heard that, men. Start praying! *(They go off like a hideous parody of the Crucifixion)* Right, prayers over. Someone give us the song of the old hermit of Chartres.

REBEL I'll sing it. I've written new words for it. *(He sings)*

There was an old hermit of Chartres
Who fell in love with a tartre.
The cunning old fox
Contracted the pox
And became a good Christian martre.
Alleluia! Alle-lu-ia!

(They disappear. The Arabic trumpet sounds a louder and more imminent note)

ARCHBISHOP *(To the* WIFE*)* Come with me. Do not stand here, staring into the distance. What can you see, child?

WIFE I'll tell you soon enough.

(There is a sound of the clash of arms, shrieks and screams. It rises to an electronic intensity and dies on a sob. The victor appears. He was known as the ENEMY LEADER *in Roman times. He is now in the gorgeous robes of an Arab chieftain. With him is his daughter, veiled. He claps his hands. A couple of Arabs carry in the suit of armor and set it down)*

ENEMY LEADER *(Tapping the armor with his scimitar)* Are you still in there, Christian? You have had the incalculable misfortune to fall into the hands of the Emir Ibrahim Bin Yussuf Al Hadj, the richest of your opponents, and the most devout. *(The* GENERAL *enters. He wears only a loincloth, and his hands are tied. He looks minute alongside his Armor.* THE UNKNOWN SOLDIER *enters with him, also tied)* Oh, there you are! How you have shrunk in defeat, little fellow.

GENERAL I am Archibald, Count of Rochentière.

ENEMY LEADER *(Sarcastic)* Who would have thought it.

GENERAL A ransom can be arranged.

ENEMY LEADER Not with me. No money can speak for you. *(Curious)* Ah, after all, you have one soldier with you who did not run away. Do you plead for your leader's life, fellow?

THE UNKNOWN SOLDIER Yes, I plead for any man's life.

ENEMY LEADER *(Staring at him)* But I know you . . . not so much your face as your expression . . . Yasmina, my daughter, do you remember him?

WOMAN *(Unsure)* No . . .

ENEMY LEADER A tree . . . a tree beside a mountain path . . . we passed in chains, you and I . . . a couple of Roman soldiers staring at the sky like lovers . . . *(He turns slowly to the* GENERAL, *snarling)* And you! Three times round the walls of Rome . . . now I know you! Showered with rose petals by that belching, puking, stinking Roman mob! The rocks and pebbles hammering my head. I hoped that every second would be my last, but still I lived on.

GENERAL Stop it! Those were different times . . .

ENEMY LEADER *(Full of loathing)* Different times!

GENERAL There were no great moral issues. We all behaved like animals. We knew no better.

ENEMY LEADER Did we not? I asked you whether you believed in a life after death and you mocked me. Now have you learned to believe? I still do, alas. I cannot kill you for ever!

(He lunges at the GENERAL. THE UNKNOWN SOLDIER *steps forward)*

THE UNKNOWN SOLDIER No! *(He accepts the blow on the shoulder and sinks to the ground)* No more death . . .

(He dies)

WIFE Now try to console me.

ARCHBISHOP I look into your eyes, and see that I cannot.

WIFE No, you cannot . . .

(She exits slowly)

ARCHBISHOP *(He vanishes)* Oh my God, to what folly have I lent your name?

ENEMY LEADER *(Slow)* You have found a man to die for you, and it has appeased my anger. Who was he?

GENERAL *(Shaking)* I never knew his name.

ENEMY LEADER *(With opulent Oriental melancholy)* With what economy he expressed himself, and made us look like fools! We will build a fountain from which fresh water will play eternally. Our finest craftsmen will encrust it with rubies and emeralds, symbolizing blood and hope. It will be known as the fountain of the Unknown Warrior, the words "No more death" will be inscribed upon it, and it will be a place of pilgrimage.

GENERAL All this for a simple soldier?

ENEMY LEADER (*With a return of cunning*) All this for a simple soldier. And for the Count? What did he do to you after I had been taken to Rome, Yasmina?

WOMAN He respected me for a day or two.

ENEMY LEADER How strange—and then?

WOMAN Then he took me to his bed after all.

ENEMY LEADER He made you his wife?

WOMAN No. He sold me into slavery. He had a wife already.

ENEMY LEADER I see. He likes many women, as we do. The life of the harem would suit him down to the ground, don't you think?

GENERAL I have all the women I want in my castle.

ENEMY LEADER Did nobody warn you that it is dangerous to refuse the hospitality of an Arab? We are extremely sensitive people. Generosity is a part of our religion. I invite you to share my harem with me for life.

GENERAL I am, of course, profoundly touched.

ENEMY LEADER As a eunuch.

GENERAL You must be joking!

ENEMY LEADER I am prepared to laugh, Christian. Take him away! (*The Arabs bustle the screaming* GENERAL *out. The* ENEMY LEADER *laughs*) Is the joke a good one, Yasmina?

WOMAN Very good, O my father, but I can't help wondering . . .

ENEMY LEADER Yes?

WOMAN What will he do to you next time?

ENEMY LEADER (*Nervous, for once*) You are right, my treasure . . . (*As they go*) Once he is castrated, we must treat him with every consideration. (*The* GENERAL *screams*) Oh, my dear Count, you will partake of some sherbet with me?

(*The sky darkens again. The men wander on, disheveled, in rags*)

SERGEANT Where are we?

REBEL It's cold now . . . we must be near home . . .

(*The* ARCHBISHOP *appears, now dressed as a Puritan, with conical black hat, austere coat and pumps. He carries a small portable pulpit, which he erects*)

SERGEANT Beg pardon, sir, could you tell us where we are?

ARCHBISHOP Thou art lost, thee and thine.

35914 We know we're lost, with all due respect. We'd like to know where we are.

ARCHBISHOP Upon the road to redemption, if thou wilt hear my lesson.

14768 Redemption? In what land is that?

ARCHBISHOP In the kingdom of heaven.

35914 We don't want to go there, sir. We've managed to avoid that.

ARCHBISHOP Thou standeth in need of salvation, brother. We have sinned exceedingly, and there is no health in us. The coffers of righteousness are empty, the vaults of Satan full to overflowing. Let us begin our war upon the master of darkness at the beginning, at the hour of birth. The newborn child must needs be covered at once, lest the sight of his own nakedness lead him into immediate temptation . . . at times of lactation, the dress should be so arranged that only the nipple protrudeth, never seeming to be the crown of that odious rotundity which is the field for some of Beelzebub's most notorious pranks. The infant should be blindfolded, and guided to the milk-giving valve, so that no heinous association may develop in later life. I see a question?

SERGEANT May it please Your Honor, we're just a platoon of soldiers on our way home from the Crusades. If you'd just answer our question, we'll be on our way . . .

(The entire cast begins to assemble during the ARCHBISHOP*'s harangue. They are dressed simply, and without palpable personality)*

ARCHBISHOP *(Aghast)* From the Crusades, sayest thou? Repent, repent then! Monstrous instruments of a Popish plot! And home, say you? Home is the world for Christian brothers. In my company, thou art in the company of almighty God, and therefore thou art home!

(The men look at one another in perplexity)

14768 Home is where my wife and children are.

ARCHBISHOP What sayest thou? And would'st thou do with thy wife, pray?

14768 If you must know, I would lay with her . . . it's been about twenty years . . . I enjoy her company . . .

ARCHBISHOP Lay with her? My brother, the devil is well and truly entrenched in thee! Out, out I say!

14768 Out what?

ARCHBISHOP Out, Satan! Our sisters are in this world for the sacred purpose of procreation, and no other—at no time may they be enjoyed. *(He suddenly sees the* WIFE*)* Thy ankle is showing, sister! *(A murmur of anger rises among the crowd)* Thou never knowest where Satan will show himself next!

REBEL (*With a shout*) We *are* home! It's Father Benedict! He's gone 'round the bend!

SERGEANT (*Angry*) Don't you know better than to interrupt a sermon?

REBEL Father Benedict! The bird with two livers! Is this the result of your guilty conscience?

(*The men seem about to manhandle the* REBEL)

ARCHBISHOP Yeah! Yeah, remind me of my sins, brother. I carry the sins of the world upon my back, among them mine own! Let him speak! It is good to suffer so!

REBEL And he's taking you in again?

14768 Stone him!

71696 Hang him!

SERGEANT Burn him! The devil's got inside him!

ARCHBISHOP Leave him be! Let us sing a hymn, in unison. Harmony too is the work of Satan, to say nothing of counterpoint, canon and fugue. Those rocky protuberances of music are ledges upon which the dark one can conceal himself unmolested! We have the sins of centuries to erase, dearly beloved! The debit of the human race is such that it will take all our courage and all our gravity to rediscover the paradise we have lost. Take heart! Cover the statues, whitewash the churches, dress the naked on the murals, and above all—above all—close the theaters—for ever!

(*The entire cast, who have placed Puritan hats on their heads during this speech, and murmured "Amens" and "Alleluias," now gaze upward as the curtain slowly falls. Their eyes follow the curtain with awe and a bewildered sense of occasion*)

Curtain

SECOND ACT OF WAR

The stage has an atmosphere of cool precision about it, and no wonder, for the ARCHBISHOP *sits there sipping chocolate, his ample wig cascading down his shoulders. He is enjoying the company of the beautiful female who has been known hitherto as simply the* WOMAN.

WOMAN How is it, my Lord Archbishop, that, apart from your wig, which betokens adherence to another age, there is nothing about you to suggest the thinker, let alone the divine?

ARCHBISHOP (*Affable*) La, madam, we live in the Age of Reason. In an age of reason, it behooves men to behave reasonably.

WOMAN Men, yes, but clergymen?

ARCHBISHOP Clerygymen most of all, for they have the reputation of being the least reasonable of men. Have you not noticed how they rail against common practices such as adultery?

WOMAN Would you defend libertines then?

ARCHBISHOP Are not the words liberty and libertine derived from the same source, madam? Does not indeed libertine have a feminine grace to it, leaving liberty but a pallid masculinity—yet we, cowardly creatures that we are, tend to lay down our lives for the one and condemn the other.

WOMAN Are you not afraid of being overheard, my Lord?

ARCHBISHOP By women? I ask nothing better. By men? I am a man. By other clerics? I waited until I was at the top of my particular tree before I gave free rein to my thoughts. (*He sighs humorously*) And thus I wasted the best years of my life. (*Smiling*) Do I confuse you? May I make amends by complimenting you upon your chocolate? It is as delectable as you are.

WOMAN Is that a declaration, sir, or an expression of regret?

ARCHBISHOP (*Aside*) With that wit she reads between my lines—although I must say, the spaces I leave there are enormous. I will dissemble. (*To the* WOMAN) Were I to be over-conscious of the gray hairs which lie concealed beneath this wig, then I own, madam, it would be an expression of regret. And yet, if I am to pay heed to the youthful heart which still lies hidden beneath the cloth, I'll grant it is a declaration.

WOMAN (*Aside*) Vanity knows no age. As man's body weakens, it is the only one of his attributes which grows stronger by the minute.

ARCHBISHOP May I have some more chocolate?

WOMAN (*Aside*) His desires are insatiable. And yet, if the younger clerics were like he, the churches would be full to overflowing. (*She rings a bell*) Sir, how did you come by such light thoughts?

ARCHBISHOP I came to them by artistry, madam, for nothing requires more art in its diffusion than conventional morality. For example, I make you conscious of your own morality, madam, by compelling you to reject my advances.

WOMAN And if I surrender to you, sir?

ARCHBISHOP Then I will happily admit failure, madam,

and pray for better luck next time. Come, shall we to your bedchamber?

WOMAN But I have ordered more chocolate, sir!

ARCHBISHOP After I have drunk my chocolate, madam.

(The WIFE *enters, carrying the chocolate. She is a plump and appetizing soubrette)*

WOMAN You speak with a rare cynicism, my Lord.

ARCHBISHOP Madam, it is the language of our times. The Puritans sought to bend the world into the image of paradise, but being human, all they succeeded in doing was to emulate hell. The great wind of freedom which sweeps through the world is mankind's sigh of relief . . . relief at life rediscovered . . . with all its transitory pleasures and teasing condiments.

WOMAN *(Aside)* With what indecent haste he drinks his beverage! I must induce him to ask for a third cup.

ARCHBISHOP *(Aside)* That is, without a doubt, the worst chocolate I have drunk in years. What sacrifices a man must make to punctuate his gallantry, for the greatest enemy of the rake is haste.

WOMAN Will you not partake of another cup, sir?

ARCHBISHOP Another cup, madam, would be to abuse your time and my taste buds. Chocolate, like love, palls when taken in excessive doses. *(Rising)* Shall we then pass from one to the other?

(A bugle blows as the ARCHBISHOP *leans over his quarry)*

WOMAN It is my husband, with his regiment.

ARCHBISHOP How like a soldier, to be forever in the wrong place at the wrong time.

(The GENERAL *enters in a bright and preposterous uniform)*

GENERAL Madam, I have returned!

WOMAN And I, sir, am the happiest and most impatient of women!

GENERAL (*Seizing her, with a laugh*) Impatient, say you?

WOMAN (*Rejecting him*) To hear your news.

GENERAL Fifty days' march across Flanders and back again in search of the enemy—and no sign of him.

ARCHBISHOP He, no doubt, spent fifty days in search of you.

GENERAL Ah, my Lord Archbishop, I did not see you. (*Aside*) What does this scurvy cleric here?

ARCHBISHOP (*Aside*) If he fails to see me in a room, is it any wonder he has difficulty finding the enemy in the whole of Flanders?

GENERAL It is a strange kind of war indeed, with no sign of the enemy.

ARCHBISHOP Shall we say it is a safe kind of war?

GENERAL Is that an insinuation, sir?

ARCHBISHOP It is a congratulation, sir.

GENERAL If you were an officer . . .

ARCHBISHOP I am not, sir; I oppose graver dangers.

GENERAL Such as constipation from too much chocolate?

ARCHBISHOP Constipation of the body, sir, is curable. That of the mind, not.

GENERAL (*Aside*) This fellow rails with a spirit something less than sacred. (*To the* ARCHBISHOP) Have you designs upon my wife, sir?

ARCHBISHOP (*Aside*) For coarseness of expression, this varlet takes the wafer. (*To the* GENERAL) Not to have designs upon your wife, sir, were to be insensitive to beauty. And yet, not all designs become cathedrals.

WOMAN (*Aside*) I blush—for the cathedrals.

GENERAL Why do you blush, madam?

WOMAN Alas, sir, is it a pleasant lot for a woman of quality to know that when her husband makes reference to the enemy, he is alluding to none other than her own dear father?

GENERAL (*Rattled*) Madam, madam, we have explored this territory many times before, and found it sterile. The fact that your revered father, the King, and I find ourselves opposed on the field of battle is but one of many inconveniences which arise from a marriage of convenience. (*A trumpet sounds*) What is that?

ARCHBISHOP (*Shading his eyes and looking out over the audience*) The enemy at last! *He* has found *you.*

GENERAL (*Drawing his sword*) Outnumbered—and surprised!

ARCHBISHOP That you are surprised is never surprising.

WOMAN (*Tragic*) Father! O that this woman's heart of mine would break! To see the noblest of men locked in mortal combat!

GENERAL What's this? How how? A white flag? Does he surrender?

WOMAN Surrender! Never! Father, rather die than see your honor smirched by the vile upstart I call husband by your Royal decree!

(*The father, the* ENEMY LEADER, *enters in a uniform of absurd dignity, feathers all over the place.* THE UNKNOWN SOLDIER *carries his bag*)

ARCHBISHOP (*Since the* GENERAL *and the* WIFE *still look out over the audience*) Ahem. At the risk of surprising you again—His Majesty is with us.

ENEMY LEADER I come in peace, most elevated, splendid and resourceful Prince.

WOMAN Father!

GENERAL Silence, woman! Most noble, august and utterly serene Majesty, is this then surrender?

ENEMY LEADER Surrender? Never!

WOMAN (*Grateful*) Oh, Father!

ENEMY LEADER Silence, girl!

GENERAL Is it the gesture of men of honor to appear in line of battle at the hour of lunch?

ENEMY LEADER Let no man say I cut short meals in pursuit of glory. On this occasion, however, our interests coincide, and under the flag of truce I came as quickly as I could.

GENERAL (*Surprised*) Our interests coincide? How's this? Explain yourself, Your Majesty.

ENEMY LEADER I am aware that on the face of it, there is no love lost between us.

WOMAN Oh, Father!

GENERAL and ENEMY LEADER Silence!

ENEMY LEADER We both claim the throne of Helgoland, the electorate of Potsdam, and the morganatic Grand-Duchy of Hessen-Essen and Plessen. Pleasant as this war of succession has been, it is time to put an end to it by mutual consent before it puts an end to us by force of circumstances. I have since discovered, however, that our patrols met on numerous occasions without our knowledge.

Melissa C. Murphy as the WIFE and Christopher Walken as THE UNKNOWN SOLDIER.

GENERAL What say you?

ENEMY LEADER They met, and in lieu of killing each other as prescribed in the articles of war, they fraternized, comparing notes on conditions of life, payment, and the like.

GENERAL Have you proof of this?

ENEMY LEADER This man, my servant. Come forward, man. (*To the* GENERAL) Speak slowly, he is a fool.

GENERAL (*Very slowly*) Is this true, man? Did you fraternize with my soldiers? (*Pause*) Make friends? (*Pause*) Pow-wow?

THE UNKNOWN SOLDIER (*Grinning*) Oh yes, sir, we did, but not more than once or twice a day. There wasn't the opportunity, you see.

GENERAL And why did you not tell your officers of this?

THE UNKNOWN SOLDIER We reckoned they'd have put a stop to it.

GENERAL (*Exploding*) But why is this man still alive? He should have been shot as an example!

ENEMY LEADER Are you willing to shoot your entire army as an example if you are not sure that I am going to do likewise?

GENERAL (*Suddenly*) But I know you, soldier. You always went off and chatted with the enemy, didn't you?

THE UNKNOWN SOLDIER I've always been interested in people, sir, if that's what you mean.

GENERAL And flowers . . . and poetry . . .

ENEMY LEADER (*Dry*) He died for you once, and now you wish to shoot him.

GENERAL Great heavens, I know you too!

WOMAN (*Suffering*) I warned you, Father.

GENERAL The degradation of a life spent in a smelly harem, surrounded by vast women bathing in curdled milk!

ENEMY LEADER You used to sing for us after supper in a pure and exquisite coloratura voice.

(*With a roar, the* GENERAL *draws his sword. The* ENEMY LEADER *does likewise*)

WOMAN Father! Husband!

ENEMY LEADER Do keep quiet, Annabel. Your relationship to us has been established quite a while ago. (*To the* GENERAL) I recognized you at your wedding, dog!

GENERAL Why did you allow me to go through with it?

ENEMY LEADER Because the world has shrunk. A king needs enemies to justify his appetite for conquest—and what greater evidence of esteem is there than to keep enmity in the family. I could think of no greater compliment to you.

GENERAL You were afraid of me this time! That's why you bribed me with your daughter.

ENEMY LEADER (*Haughty*) It is ungentlemanly to draw attention to the truth in such a cavalier fashion.

GENERAL It's true then!

ENEMY LEADER I only admit it because the days of our hostility are over, as are the days of elegance in battle. (*They resheathe their swords*) This business of stopping battles for meals, which began as an exquisite courtesy, has become an acute embarrassment. There is not enough bread to go round—and in the absence of bread, the only substitute is thought.

WOMAN If there is no bread, let them eat—

(*She stops abruptly*)

ARCHBISHOP What, my daughter?

WOMAN I was going to say something dreadful.

ARCHBISHOP Rest assured—it has already been said.

ENEMY LEADER Our soldiers have begun to read. We encouraged them in our infinite blindness—believing in a kind of abstract enlightenment as a mark of progress. But—sooner than you imagine—mark my words—they will master thoughts as well, ideas, theories. And how will a decent war be possible with literate soldiery?

GENERAL You're mad! A soldier with theories?

ENEMY LEADER (*To* THE UNKNOWN SOLDIER) Who is your favorite author, man?

THE UNKNOWN SOLDIER I don't know many, Your Majesty.

ENEMY LEADER But you can read?

THE UNKNOWN SOLDIER Slowly, Your Majesty. I still confuse the effs and the esses.

ENEMY LEADER And have you any preferences as to reading matter?

THE UNKNOWN SOLDIER Oh yes, Your Majesty. But there's still so much I haven't read, I don't like to express myself.

ENEMY LEADER Feel free, man, feel free.

THE UNKNOWN SOLDIER Well, Your Majesty, if that's an order—then, I'd say, of the little I have read, I like Voltaire best of all.

GENERAL (*Staggered*) Voltaire?

WOMAN Voltaire? Who's that?

ENEMY LEADER Quiet, Annabel. You are too well educated to know. (*To* THE UNKNOWN SOLDIER) And do you understand him?

THE UNKNOWN SOLDIER No, sir, not entirely. That's perhaps why I like him. I am compelled to read him again and again, Your Majesty.

ENEMY LEADER And what book in particular is your favorite? There's hardly room in your pack to take the collected works into battle.

THE UNKNOWN SOLDIER Oh, a little volume, Your Majesty—I hope I pronounce it right—called *Can-deed.*

GENERAL (*Exploding*) Where did you get it?

THE UNKNOWN SOLDIER One of your soldiers was kind enough to lend it me, sir, on patrol. Now that I've finished it, I hope to be able to return it to him, if we're lucky enough to go on patrol again.

GENERAL (*Beside himself*) What kind of book is this *Candide?*

ENEMY LEADER (*Amused*) You have not read it?

GENERAL (*Stoutly*) I have read about it. That is why I have not read it.

ENEMY LEADER It is about the victory of a simpleton over the hazards of a world governed by kings, princes and prelates. I will lend you a copy.

ARCHBISHOP (*Dryly*) I have a copy here.

(*The* GENERAL *seizes it*)

ENEMY LEADER We must sign the peace treaty without delay. Already our men are intermingling on the parade ground.

GENERAL (*Looking out over the audience*) Exchanging reading matter! (*Furious*) My court of honor looks like the campus of a university! What's come over them? They're even laughing! Let us adjourn to the apartments of state. Madam, do you partake of some chocolate with His Lordship while your royal father and I do draft the treaty.

ARCHBISHOP (*As they go*) More chocolate! Six more cups and she'll be mine!

(*When they have gone,* THE UNKNOWN SOLDIER *avidly opens his pack, brings out a slim volume, and sits down to read it, slowly, with fiendish application. He understands a phrase with the greatest difficulty, and roars with laughter. The* WIFE *enters with a tray to take away the chocolate*)

WIFE (*Robust*) Get up off the good chair, you lout! (*They look at one another.* THE UNKNOWN SOLDIER *slowly rises. Long pause. Her voice is small, with ill-disguised emotion*) Oh, it's you . . .

THE UNKNOWN SOLDIER (*Awkward*) After all this time, is that all you're going to say?

WIFE What do you expect me to do? Rush into your arms?

THE UNKNOWN SOLDIER (*Almost inaudible*) I half-expected it, I must say.

WIFE What are you doing, dressed up like that?

THE UNKNOWN SOLDIER I'm a subject of His Majesty.

WIFE Since when?

THE UNKNOWN SOLDIER All my life, all this life.

WIFE What are you doing? Reading?

THE UNKNOWN SOLDIER Mm.

WIFE That's new.

THE UNKNOWN SOLDIER It's new, yes. Five years ago it was only the alphabet. Now it's every other word, sometimes two in three. Can you read?

WIFE I can write my name.

THE UNKNOWN SOLDIER That's a start. (*Pause*) What are you doing here?

WIFE I'm in service with the Prince—or rather, with the Princess. We hardly ever see the Prince.

THE UNKNOWN SOLDIER Well, it was bound to happen, I suppose.

WIFE What?

THE UNKNOWN SOLDIER Our meeting again. (*Pause*) Remember we used to spout poetry at each other? I can't do it any more. Since I started reading, I can't phrase a thought properly, the way I used to.

WIFE I don't want to remember it.

THE UNKNOWN SOLDIER Why not?

WIFE I was someone else then, I was younger.

THE UNKNOWN SOLDIER No, you weren't.

WIFE I was younger. That's why I can't bring myself to rush into your arms.

THE UNKNOWN SOLDIER Don't you want to?

WIFE God knows I want to.
(*They embrace*)

THE UNKNOWN SOLDIER What's the matter?

WIFE We're an old married couple, that's what's the matter. We're an old married couple at birth, every time, every time . . . and you keep on getting yourself killed. I can't keep up with you, and that's the truth. It's too silly.

THE UNKNOWN SOLDIER You may be right. But I'm a bit slow, you know. I need time to think things over.

WIFE Time? Centuries.

THE UNKNOWN SOLDIER Centuries is time.

WIFE What's your name now?

THE UNKNOWN SOLDIER Engelbrecht.

WIFE Serves you right.

THE UNKNOWN SOLDIER What's yours?

WIFE Ernestine.

THE UNKNOWN SOLDIER That's pretty.

WIFE You know it's hideous. (*She rushes into his arms*) Oh God, how you annoy me!

(*They kiss*)

THE UNKNOWN SOLDIER Thank heaven I've found you.

WIFE Thank heaven, yes, but for how long? You're bound to do something stupid again.

THE UNKNOWN SOLDIER I don't consciously do stupid things.

WIFE D'you think I'd love you if you weren't what you are? You'll go under again when I'm six months gone. And I'll be hawking your child around, begging for alms.

THE UNKNOWN SOLDIER What's he like?

WIFE Who?

THE UNKNOWN SOLDIER Our son.

WIFE How d'you know it's a son?

THE UNKNOWN SOLDIER Stands to reason. It's me that needs replacing, not you.

WIFE He's fine. Sometimes he's thin and undernourished,

sometimes he's huge and demanding. Last time he insisted on being breast-fed until he was two years old. It was agony. But always he's the spitting image of you —with that soft and welcoming look—and I'm beginning to think that I'm a fool to go through these endless labor pains just in order to bring forth another one—a lad who will one day go into his father's business—that of being an unknown soldier.

THE UNKNOWN SOLDIER (*Trying to be bright*) Oh, come on, I'm not ready to retire yet.

WIFE That's the trouble.

THE UNKNOWN SOLDIER (*Sighs*) I reckon someone's got to do it, once it's become an established practice. Like someone's got to be the hangman. It's unpleasant, but someone's got to do it while there's hanging.

WIFE (*Very wistful*) The hangman comes home for supper. (*She sees his dejected look at the irrefutability of her argument, and is moved*) Oh, come with me to my room . . . I need you in my arms, you fool!

THE UNKNOWN SOLDIER When?

WIFE Now!

THE UNKNOWN SOLDIER But I'm on duty.

WIFE So am I.

(*A song begins to swell in volume as men and flags and lanterns begin to appear*)

CHORUS (*Singing*)

Lift up your eyes, and face the light,
You men accustomed to the night.
The scarlet banner of revolt has burst
Through the cloudbanks of despair.

(*As the menace increases,* THE UNKNOWN SOLDIER *and his* WIFE *seek comfort from one another*)

WIFE I hate it when men sing together. It's always a sign of going away.

THE UNKNOWN SOLDIER I don't recognize the music—or the words.

CHORUS *(Singing)*

Lift up your eyes, prepare to fight.
Freedom's torch is burning bright.
Snuff out the lives of the accurs'd,
Hold their heads up by the hair!

(The men burst in)

71696 *(A new personality)* Where's your revolutionary cap, citizen?

THE UNKNOWN SOLDIER *(Laughing)* Why don't you call me by my name then?

94343 Our names keep us apart in the shadow of religion and superstition. The name of citizen unites us in secular equality.

WIFE *(Nervous)* Come with me. We've got some work to do.

14768 What work is more pressing than revolution, citizen? (THE UNKNOWN SOLDIER *laughs)* Why do you laugh?

THE UNKNOWN SOLDIER At your joke, friend. It so happens my most pressing work is to press His Majesty's shirts.

(There is an outcry among the men)

REBEL *(Calming the fury of the men)* Do it then, albeit for the last time. Revenge is good and wholesome, but to degrade the condemned would be merely savage. Let kings die in spotless linen. It is the only perfection they know.

THE UNKNOWN SOLDIER *(Annoyed)* What's all this talk about kings dying? What are you lads up to?

WIFE Come away from here, Engelbrecht.

THE UNKNOWN SOLDIER No. I've got to get to the bottom of this.

REBEL The revolution has swept away centuries of tradition in the blinking of an eye, in the changing of a thought, in the twinge of a nerve. We took even ourselves by surprise. For the first time in history, the people have seized the power nature intended as their birthright! Now before we build the new life on the eroded soil of society, we must dispose of the garbage from the banquet of kings and emperors which has come to an end at last!

(The men cheer and harangue him)

THE UNKNOWN SOLDIER It's all wrong, you know, to do all this without asking!

REBEL *(Powerful, staying the fury of the men)* Take him away, woman, and let him into your secrets. He is so overwrought that, if you do not turn his passion in your direction, he may well overthrow the revolution by himself.

(The men's anger is canalized into laughter)

WIFE *(Pulling at* THE UNKNOWN SOLDIER*)* Come on. Come away.

14768 *(Who is not so easily sidetracked)* I demand his head!

REBEL *(Patient)* You will have it, citizen, I have no doubt. But in time. Let us concentrate on heads with brains in them. Where is the captive? *(The* INVENTOR *comes on in chains)* Ah. The citizens arrested you in your workshop, I understand. You were building a cannon for the King and a new type of breech-loading rifle for the Prince. You were serving two masters.

INVENTOR (*Scornful*) He who serves only one master is a slave; he who serves two is already relatively free.

REBEL There is a degree of logic in your cynicism.

INVENTOR On the contrary, there is a degree of cynicism in my logic. I have chains on my wrists. Why? The men who judge me until yesterday fired the rifles I designed, whichever side they were on. There is no difference in morality between us, only a difference in salary.

REBEL (*Powerful*) You cannot blame a working-man for wishing to eat.

INVENTOR (*Powerful*) And you cannot blame an intellectual for wishing to eat more than the working-man!

71696 (*Furious*) I demand his head!

REBEL What are your terms for working for us?

71696 (*In the outcry*) He should die, and now you're freeing him?

REBEL To kill him will serve no purpose except to put an end to years of research and knowledge which we can use. I ask you, citizens, to close your minds to the ugly thoughts this creature expresses.

INVENTOR (*Released*) My terms are to free me of my shackles. I don't even insist that you put them on yourselves. *Now* tell me I am incapable of generosity!

REBEL Kindly stick to technicalities at all times. Free this citizen!

14768 (*Obeying*) I think it's revolting.

REBEL Rest assured, citizen, I agree with you.

71696 Then why . . .

REBEL (*Violent*) Because there are a hundred other

kings left. We have only set one foot in the door of the vast ballroom of state. Shall we rub our hands in self-congratulation and talk of world revolution when all but the first small gesture remains yet to be made? Where we had one enemy before, we now have countless enemies. And he will win who walks forward with the purity of his ideals in one hand and science in the other!

INVENTOR Admirably expressed, if I may say so.

REBEL What have you for us?

INVENTOR An idea I have cherished for some years, and held back against the rainy day, as it were. It came back to me owing to the crowded condition of my cell. This . . . (*He spreads out his plan*) . . . device is a semi-automatic decapitator which is able to sever five heads every eight minutes during a normal working day. This represents a figure of three hundred and twenty victims in a working day or two thousand two hundred and forty a week. I don't know if it's your intention to work on Sundays.

REBEL There will be a day of rest—on any day but Sunday. Have you made provision for the trials in your assessment?

INVENTOR (*A little disappointed*) Oh, there are to be trials? I see . . . (*Ingratiating and apologetic*) Naturally, I couldn't take trials into my calculations, which are of a necessarily abstract and technical nature.

REBEL (*Puzzled*) This invention of yours reminds me of something.

INVENTOR (*Hasty*) Oh, I know it bears a superficial resemblance to a French contraption, but theirs does not go far enough. It only dislodges one head at a time. Owing to the extreme rigidity of my frame and the length of my blade, I can dislodge five at a time. There is no comparison between the two humane exterminators. (*Suddenly mournful*) Yet, life is never without its ironies. The simple fact that the revolution broke out in France and not here means that my device will go into the history books as a guillotine and not as a Schwalbenbrecher.

REBEL I understand your deception, citizen.

INVENTOR It is wonderful to be understood . . . (*Risking it*) citizen?

REBEL Take your places at the bench. The republican court is now in session.

INVENTOR (*Sotto voce*) You mean, I was not on trial? Then, with your permission, I will go to my workshop to prepare!

REBEL (*The* WIFE *enters. She is pregnant*) Are you on trial, citizen? If so, take your place in the dock.

WIFE (*Anxious*) I'm not on trial, but I heard a rumor my man was.

REBEL Rumors these days are usually correct. You may be seated if you wish to see justice dispensed.

WIFE But . . . don't you remember me?

REBEL (*Cold*) Yes, I remember you.

WIFE My man saved your life!

REBEL You expect me to save his? I am not a man any longer, but an instrument of the people's justice. Take a seat if you wish. Enter the dock, Archbishop.

(*The* ARCHBISHOP *is led on*)

94343 On a point of order! Is it not citizen Archbishop?

REBEL He will be citizen Archbishop if acquitted. If not, he will remain plain Archbishop, and an enemy of the people.

ARCHBISHOP It is strange that today a friend of God should by definition be an enemy of the people.

REBEL God does not exist.

ARCHBISHOP Since when?

REBEL Since yesterday at the tenth hour, when Decree 914 of the Republican Code was passed unanimously.

ARCHBISHOP I see. Well, it's just as well to know this.

71696 Reason is the only God.

ARCHBISHOP So there is a God after all, if it is Reason. Strange still that if Reason be God, that a man of Reason should be an enemy of the people.

REBEL (*To* 71696. *Irritated*) Citizen, await your turn to speak. You have no experience in argument.

71696 (*Dogged*) Citizen, I know my rights.

ARCHBISHOP (*Aside*) To know one's rights is one thing. To exercise them, quite another. I fear our friend is not long for this committee, or for this world.

REBEL Are you an Archbishop?

ARCHBISHOP I am.

REBEL Do you believe in God?

ARCHBISHOP I do. (*A buzz of excitement among the committee members*) Is it so surprising to find an Archbishop who believes in God?

REBEL Are you willing, from this day on, to accept Reason as your God?

ARCHBISHOP Certainly. I see nothing incompatible between God and Reason. God has never required me to do other than to behave reasonably.

REBEL Are you prepared to desecrate your altars, to strip your abbey of all religious symbols?

ARCHBISHOP In that most religious symbols are inferior art, I will not weep to see them go. If you really feel that the people have overnight attained such a degree of mental sophistication that we can dispense with all Christian symbolism, I am quite willing to attempt the experiment.

94343 Why do you give in to our ideas so easily? Are you afraid of death?

ARCHBISHOP (*Smiling*) Of course I am afraid of death. I am only a man, after all—and that's why I'm gratified that I have not had to give in, as you say, to a single one of your ideas. I have not even compromised. You have not required me to. It would have been different if you had asked me to believe in *nothing*. You have not done so, precisely because you know full well that you cannot ask the people to believe in *nothing*. They will not follow you if you do. You must cautiously transfer their belief from one deity to another, and if I arrive at the conclusion that the two deities are, in fact, the same one, I see no reason to quarrel with you. You may think you are desecrating; all you are really doing is redecorating.

94343 Are you accusing us of being Christians then?

ARCHBISHOP I would not dream of being so impolite, citizen. I am merely saying that we are, all of us, reasonable.

REBEL (*Smiling in spite of himself*) Thank you, citizen. I move for his immediate acquittal. All citizens in favor kindly signify your approval in the usual manner.

71696 I ask for death.

94343 I second that.

35914 No opinion.

14768 No opinion.

REBEL You are acquitted.

ARCHBISHOP Thank you very much.

71696 I protest!

REBEL As chairman, I have the casting vote under Clause 8, Subsection 24 A.

94343 You have no right . . .

REBEL There is no time for technicalities, we have work to do, citizen! (*He raps his gavel*) Next prisoner. (*The* ARCHBISHOP *sits beside the* WIFE, *who moves away slightly. The* ENEMY LEADER *enters. He is bound*) What is your profession?

ENEMY LEADER King.

REBEL Do you repent?

ENEMY LEADER What for, you scum? For being what I was born?

94343 (*Rising, furious*) What's that he called us?

ENEMY LEADER My time is valuable. Don't waste it. Where do I go to die?

REBEL You will be told soon enough. Have you anything to say?

ENEMY LEADER A great deal, but not to you. Now kindly take my head off. There are ladies waiting.

REBEL Do you require religious consolation according to your beliefs?

ENEMY LEADER As a king, I can offer it myself.

REBEL Are we unanimous? (*Nobody dares to stir*) Death. Stand aside there.

ENEMY LEADER Thank you for your courteous brevity.

REBEL Next prisoner. (*As the* ENEMY LEADER *steps aside,*

the GENERAL, *now the Prince, enters the dock)* What is your profession?

GENERAL You know perfectly well.

REBEL Do you repent?

GENERAL Why? You think it easy to rule? *(He laughs)* Good luck to you all—and I thank you, gentlemen, for taking a weight off my shoulders—get it? A weight off my shoulders?

(He and the ENEMY LEADER *laugh heartily)*

ENEMY LEADER Damn good. I must remember that. Weight off my shoulders.

(The GENERAL *steps down)*

REBEL We have not finished with you yet!

GENERAL I have finished with you, however.

94343 *(Hysterical)* Death! Death! I won't be laughed at like that!

(This provokes renewed laughter from the monarchs)

ENEMY LEADER How did we ever fight decent wars with such animals?

REBEL *(Rapping his gavel rhythmically)* Kindly re-enter the dock!

GENERAL I refuse. You are determined to kill us. Therefore you can no longer threaten us. Please hurry up. There are already four thousand souls in a prison I built to contain sixty. Conditions there are intolerable. No doubt it is due to your administrative inexperience, but you simply must execute at the rate you arrest, otherwise there will be outbreaks of the plague, and as Prince, that is the last blight I wish on my subjects.

REBEL *(Betraying a little irritation)* We are quite aware of the problems. Do you desire religious consolation?

GENERAL (*Gay*) From the Archbishop? My wife may accept.

REBEL Death. Next prisoner. (*The* WOMAN *enters the dock. The* WIFE *gasps*) Profession?

WOMAN None.

REBEL Do you repent?

WOMAN Repent? What for? I have had an enviable life. The only fear which forever haunted me was that of old age. Now, thanks to your generosity, this fear is removed from me, for which I humbly thank you.

WIFE (*In tears*) Oh, Your Highness!

WOMAN I will not need that army of face creams, Ernestine. I bequeath them to you.

REBEL Have you anything to say?

WOMAN I am a woman, gentlemen. I have already talked excessively all my life.

REBEL Do you require religious consolation?

WOMAN I am not certain, gentlemen, that the consolation I would derive from His Lordship the Archbishop would be of a purely spiritual nature, and so, in the interest of my soul, which will presently be under more august scrutiny, I had best abstain here on earth.

(*The* GENERAL *and the* ENEMY LEADER *applaud her statement*)

GENERAL Excellent speech.

ENEMY LEADER Absolutely first class.

REBEL Death. Next prisoner. (*The* SERGEANT *takes the* WOMAN'S *place. A murmur of hostility*) Profession?

SERGEANT Sergeant, as you know full well.

REBEL Do you repent?

SERGEANT Repent? Have you lost your reason, lads, or something? I only did my duty.

94343 You struck me across the face with the butt of a blunderbuss 'cos you said I wasn't peelin' potatoes fine enough!

SERGEANT I told you to peel the shiftin' spuds, not cut them in half! I will not have waste!

94343 Four teeth lost—and teeth is harder to come by than potatoes!

14768 You kept the water from us in the desert!

71696 You stole our food from us in Greece!

REBEL (*Rapping his gavel in order to cut short the fugue*) Order! Order in the revolutionary court!

94343 Death!

14768 Death!

71696 Death!

35914 Oh, I don't know . . . it seems too late to kill him now . . . I've thought of it so often, but now—I mean, it'd be like killing a chicken you've begun to call by name, isn't it?

REBEL Have you anything to say?

SERGEANT (*In a weak voice*) Yes. Yes, I got a lot to say.

REBEL Make it brief.

SERGEANT What's come over you all? I was like a father and a mother to you all . . . when I knocked out your teeth . . . who picked them up?

94343 You did, to throw them away.

SERGEANT They was no good to you any more, was they?

14768 I'm going to vomit if he goes on.

REBEL Have you finished?

SERGEANT I haven't hardly begun.

REBEL Do you require religious consolation?

SERGEANT And another thing . . .

GENERAL Sergeant.

SERGEANT (*Stiffening*) Sah!

GENERAL Answer the question.

SERGEANT I didn't hear no question, sah!

GENERAL Do you require religious consolation?

SERGEANT I don't want to die, sah, with your permission.

GENERAL You are to die, Sergeant. That's an order.

SERGEANT Sah!

GENERAL Why are you trembling, man?

SERGEANT It's never 'appened to me before, sir.

REBEL Death. Stand down. Next prisoner.

(THE UNKNOWN SOLDIER *enters the dock*)

WIFE (*Emotional*) What are you doing there?

THE UNKNOWN SOLDIER (*Smiling*) I don't know. Ask the lads.

REBEL Profession?

THE UNKNOWN SOLDIER Soldier.

WIFE (*Violent*) What's come over you all? You know him as well as I do—better! Profession: Unknown Soldier. Why all the stupid questions? What kind of a revolution is this?

REBEL (*Rapping his gavel*) The authority of the court will be respected.

THE UNKNOWN SOLDIER (*Tapping his stomach*) You're not . . . again?

WIFE Of course I am. I always am.

THE UNKNOWN SOLDIER (*Incredulous*) That's quick.

REBEL (*Insistent*) Do you repent?

THE UNKNOWN SOLDIER What for?

REBEL I take it that is an answer. Have you anything to say?

THE UNKNOWN SOLDIER What about?

ARCHBISHOP May I intercede for him, citizen?

REBEL Can he not speak for himself, citizen?

ARCHBISHOP I think no, citizen.

94343 I object!

REBEL On what authority do you wish to intercede on his behalf?

ARCHBISHOP On the authority of Reason, citizen.

REBEL (*Laying down his quill*) Very well.

ARCHBISHOP For what crime is this man arraigned before the people's court?

REBEL That is a good question. Without such men as this, kings would be impotent, tyrants would be powerless, the revolution would have taken place long ago. Today, in this hour of triumph, when all men have rushed for their armbands and their Phrygian bonnets, he is still dressed as a soldier of the King. When arrested, he was pressing the King's shirt!

(*A murmur of anger from the court*)

ARCHBISHOP You yourself have not put a Phrygian bonnet on your head, nor are you wearing an armband. Are we to assume from that that you are less enthusiastic a revolutionary than your fellow members of the revolutionary tribunal?

REBEL I am its chairman.

ARCHBISHOP Were you always a revolutionary? Were you born one?

REBEL What do you mean?

ARCHBISHOP Wasn't there a moment at which you saw the light?

REBEL Yes, as a student.

ARCHBISHOP Well now, if this man were to choose this moment to see the light? If he were to denounce the King, for instance. Wouldn't that ensure his acquittal?

REBEL (*Smiling sadly*) Of course. But you know him as well as I do. You know very well he won't.

ARCHBISHOP (*To* THE UNKNOWN SOLDIER) Young man, you remember me.

THE UNKNOWN SOLDIER (*Smiling*) Oh yes, Your Lordship, Father Benedict, the Puritan . . .

ARCHBISHOP (*Hastily*) Yes, yes, all that. Now, I order you, as your father in God, to denounce the King. Don't ask why. Just do as I tell you. Repeat after me: I denounce the King.

THE UNKNOWN SOLDIER What for?

ARCHBISHOP You are entirely innocent. You know it. I know it. Every citizen on the revolutionary tribunal knows it. We just cannot afford to have you misunderstood once again!

35914 Go on, denounce the King!

14768 (*Edgy*) Denounce him, damn you!

THE UNKNOWN SOLDIER I don't understand what all this is about. Why are all the lads sitting up there with those hats on? Is it a new uniform, or something? Will we all be getting them?

WIFE (*Writhing*) Oh, I can see it coming again . . . For my sake . . . for our child's sake . . . denounce the King!

THE UNKNOWN SOLDIER (*Affectionate*) Don't be silly, my sweetheart. You don't even know His Majesty. How can I denounce him for your sake?

94343 (*Bursting out*) I can't stand it no more. He's always throwing himself in front of swords. Maybe that's what he wants. Let's give it him then. Death! Death! Death!

71696 He brings bad luck, that's what I say. Something always goes wrong when he turns up—something you can't forget afterward. Death!

ENEMY LEADER (*Impatient*) Come along, man, denounce me! What difference does it make now?

THE UNKNOWN SOLDIER I couldn't do that, Your Majesty, not after the great kindness you've shown me. It wouldn't be right.

ARCHBISHOP The King has ordered you to denounce him!

THE UNKNOWN SOLDIER He's no longer the King though, is he? They took him off the throne, if I understood it right. I mean, it wasn't as a king he showed me great kindness, but a man. It's as a man I owe him a lot.

REBEL (*Quiet*) Do you require religious consolation?

THE UNKNOWN SOLDIER If it'll help the Archbishop here, I'll take anything he has to offer.

ARCHBISHOP (*Faltering*) What did you say?

WIFE I want to die in his place.

REBEL You are not on trial.

WIFE I want him to know what it's like to survive! I want him to do the mourning for a change!

REBEL Sit down or leave the court.

WIFE Damn the revolution! Long live the King! There, arrest me!

REBEL (*Glacial*) You are pregnant. The death sentence may not be carried out on a pregnant woman, since you are carrying a potential revolutionary in your womb. Article 73, Subsection 18. You can shout to your heart's content, citizen. As for your husband, he has been given every chance to save himself. Either through an inability to understand the revolution or a refusal to do so, he has refused to avail himself of the opportunity. This leaves the revolutionary court no alternative but to condemn him to death. There are now sufficient criminals for the sentences to be carried out. You will be buried in a communal grave with no trace of your identities.

WIFE (*Furious*) This time he's dying before witnesses.

REBEL Order! Order!

WIFE Don't interrupt me, damn you! You know he's my husband and that I'm his wife. Even if he's to be unknown as usual—do I get my pension?

REBEL Citizen, how can you speak of money at such a time?

WIFE I've shocked you! Death of this useless sort has become a habit in our family, and anything that becomes a habit is shocking to those who face it for the first time. I want to know—and I want my man to know—do I get my pension this time as a soldier's widow?

REBEL (*Taking refuge in an unnatural calm*) There are no pensions for the dependents of criminals. You will receive the pittance due to expectant women, Article 77, and afterward free milk.

WIFE *(Screaming)* Free milk! The one thing I can produce myself, I get free! What's the difference between all your governments?

REBEL Order!

WIFE Fraternity? If my brother banged a hammer all the time I was talking to him, I'd slap his face for him, I would.

REBEL Take her away!

WIFE Take her away! So much for liberty!

WOMAN Ernestine!

WIFE *(Suddenly sober)* Yes, ma'am.

WOMAN Think of your child. You can't change anything. Go away. Let us die in peace.

(For a long while, the WOMAN *and* THE UNKNOWN SOLDIER *look at one another—a silence respected by the court. Then she goes quickly)*

REBEL Take them away.

INVENTOR *(Like a maître d'hôtel)* This way please. Now, if you will lie down here, with your face downward—in any order.

(They go off, saluting the public with bravado. The INVENTOR *remains on stage, looking off)*

ENEMY LEADER'S VOICE I refuse to lie with my face downward. What do you take me for, a slave?

INVENTOR All my calculations are based on a downward position.

ENEMY LEADER'S VOICE What are you doing, man, face downward?

THE UNKNOWN SOLDIER'S VOICE Well, I'm not a king, sir. I'm just an ordinary man.

ENEMY LEADER'S VOICE Turn over at once. That's an order!

THE UNKNOWN SOLDIER'S VOICE Yes, sir.

SERGEANT'S VOICE (*Suddenly hysterical*) I've got a new idea for my defense! I denounce the Prince! I denounce the King!

(*He is drowned in derisive voices. The* ARCHBISHOP *wanders to the front of the stage, deeply troubled. The* REBEL *joins him*)

INVENTOR Ready? A little to the left, madam. No, to your left. It won't last long. *Eins. Zwei. Drei!* (*The blade falls*) It works!

(*A cheer from the men. The next scene is punctuated by* Eins, Zwei, Drei, *the formal cheer, and the rise and fall of the blade*)

ARCHBISHOP You cannot disguise the fact that you are as troubled by events as I am.

REBEL I make no attempt to disguise anything. I believe in the revolution. That is enough.

ARCHBISHOP When will it end, this massacre of the innocents? Eins, Zwei, Drei, day after day.

REBEL It is not for me to decide. The tribunal has a communal responsibility.

ARCHBISHOP And do you think *you* will survive your responsibility?

REBEL (*Slow, smiling*) I think . . . not.

ARCHBISHOP You will be called on to die in your turn?

REBEL No doubt. The people tire of the same faces.

ARCHBISHOP And will you remain as impassive under the blade as before it?

REBEL (*Casual*) There is no life without a sense of death. Man lives his own death in his imagination all his mature life. Sometimes I die well—sometimes not so well. It will depend on the weather. But by then—there won't be much I regret leaving behind. My dog . . . the taste of coffee . . . the smell of apples . . .

ARCHBISHOP Things created by reason?

REBEL You realized yourself that we have no quarrel with God. We oppose Him merely because He has become the tool for ambitious men. It was time to liberate Him.

ARCHBISHOP Perhaps you're right.

REBEL Only perhaps?

ARCHBISHOP Doubts are the spurs of thought. The more I know what I am supposed to think, the less I know what I really think. There goes that blade again! I can hardly stand it any more!

REBEL And I hardly noticed it.

ARCHBISHOP Does that callousness signify to you that your revolution has succeeded?

REBEL It has failed.

ARCHBISHOP Then how can you pretend to support it?

REBEL And can you, as a Christian, maintain that Christianity has succeeded? (*The* ARCHBISHOP *is silent*) Ideas cannot be judged by their success or failure in practice. The idea of liberty is really only clear in captivity. Equality is only understandable in an autocracy. Fraternity has a meaning in a civil war. The poor pregnant wife was right, of course. Ideals do not lend themselves to practical application in normal times. They are vibrant only when they are unattainable.

ARCHBISHOP And love?

REBEL (*With a shrug*) Love may be possible in secret, I don't know. But on the scale of policy, it is sanctimony.

Do you love God more while preaching to a faceless multitude, or in the silence of your cloister?

ARCHBISHOP And yet there are great communal experiences.

REBEL They are political. Even Christ's miracles were political. What convinced the multitude was not a sentiment of love, but the fact that there were suddenly enough loaves and fishes to go round.

ARCHBISHOP But can we live at all if we face such facts without illusion? Do they not harden the heart? The blade falls again! You don't even flinch.

REBEL I don't even hear it. The revolution has failed, as it was bound to. And yet I am more of a revolutionary than ever. I know of no idea more beautiful, more sacred than a compulsory faith in man—who is, forever undeserving of such faith. Like you in your meditations, I knew my cause was right only when I was in isolation, waiting for the day. That longed-for day brought its compromises, the dream is tainted by the need to administer. From the pure seed of a divine idea, a political forest has sprouted.

ARCHBISHOP There is no solution, then.

REBEL You Christians are more cynical than we. Your solution is not of this world. You safely relegate it to the kingdom of heaven.

ARCHBISHOP While you aim at paradise on earth? May God help us all! As though we hadn't learned our lesson with the Puritans!

REBEL Ah yes, but we are the Puritans. Our ideals are impossible. That gives us our solemn sense of failure. Ours are the faults not of vice, but of excessive virtue. The blade has fallen again, as though to prove my point, and this time it was you that didn't hear it.

ARCHBISHOP I was frankly thinking of something else. It was the mention of the Puritans that did it.

REBEL What?

ARCHBISHOP I thought of the temptations of the flesh. I had not entertained it for so long, that it burst upon me as a new and sparkling idea. (*He sighs*) It is hard for a Christian to survive in a godless society. The first casualty in a godless society is always the devil. And without the devil, a Christian is lost . . .

(94343 *appears between them*)

94343 Citizens, you are both under arrest.

REBEL (*Unsurprised*) On what grounds, citizen?

94343 Under suspicion of having communicated with one another.

REBEL By what means?

94343 (*The most terrible of accusations*) By means of words.

ARCHBISHOP I miscalculated again. I was sure he would be the first to fall from grace.

REBEL Rest assured . . . he now holds my job . . . he will be the next.

94343 No more talking! Enter the dock. (*The* REBEL *enters the dock*) Your profession?

REBEL The saddest profession in the world. Aging revolutionary.

94343 Do you repent?

REBEL Yes. I betrayed the revolution.

94343 How?

REBEL It is for you to tell me, citizen. I have not seen the indictment.

94343 We will take that as an admission.

REBEL It was intended as one.

94343 Do you require religious consolation?

REBEL No.

94343 Have you anything to say?

REBEL (*Automatic*) Long live the glorious revolution of the people! Death to the tyrant!

94343 Death.

14768 Death.

71696 Death.

35914 Death.

94343 Next. What is your profession?

ARCHBISHOP How must I answer such questions? I no longer know. I have heard them so often, I no longer understand them. I am a man.

94343 I asked your profession, not your sex.

ARCHBISHOP I am a man. In conscience, I can't say more.

(*Two figures enter in terrifying unison, like monstrous Samurais. The one on the left is dressed in the uniform and shako of an operetta Hussar. The one on the right wears the swollen mortarboard and lifeless tassel of a Balkan lancer. The clank of metal appendages accompanies them. They both wear ferocious mustaches. They come to a noisy halt. They are the* GENERAL *and the* ENEMY LEADER)

GENERAL and ENEMY LEADER We have returned!

94343 (*Nervous*) You have no business here! Clear the court!

GENERAL (*Rasping, affected. His speech is occasionally afflicted with a distressing stammer*) Is this stupid farce still going on then? And are you still alive, Archbishop? Bravo! Although it seems we are just in time to rescue you.

ARCHBISHOP Yes, yes indeed, Your Excellencies. The nick of time, I assure you. Whom do I have the honor of addressing?

GENERAL We are the Archduke Boris-Emmanuel the Eighth.

ARCHBISHOP Both of you?

GENERAL We are using the royal "we."

ENEMY LEADER (*Who also has his speech defect—a glut of sibilants, with its attendant splashes, and a hail of saliva*) We also have that right. We are Nikolai-Ludwig of Posen and Pilsen, hereditary overlord of more places than we are able to recollect without assistance.

GENERAL We are, not unnaturally, cousins as well as brothers-in-law. We are married to one another's sisters. Our parents, too, are cousins. Everything under the sun has been done to preserve our hereditary deficiencies, which distinguish us from mere people in the singular.

ENEMY LEADER Now, hurry up, you swine, and get into uniform, where you belong! War is on the point of breaking out again.

ARCHBISHOP (*Alarmed*) War? Again? May one ask between whom?

GENERAL (*Leaning on the* ENEMY LEADER'*s shoulder*) Between us. Didn't you know, we are mortal enemies? We have seen his summer maneuvers.

ENEMY LEADER (*Smiling wickedly*) We have seen his winter maneuvers.

GENERAL (*With the same complicity*) It promises to be one of the most interesting wars yet fought.

REBEL What's the matter with you, citizens? Where's your revolutionary spirit? The court is in session, and you allow the solemn proceedings to be interrupted with only a feeble word of protest? Clear the court!

ENEMY LEADER We thought you were a prisoner?

REBEL I am under sentence of death. I insist that the sentence be carried out by the will of the people!

GENERAL Like a scorpion, this pin-headed socialist does away with himself rather than face the inexorable march of progress.

ENEMY LEADER Poor fool! Your world of high ideals is dead forever.

REBEL Once born, it can never die!

GENERAL You wish us to prove it to you? Schinkelmann!

(The INVENTOR *enters, well-dressed in the period of 1910. He wears a hard collar, pin-stripe trousers, bowler hat and pince-nez. He clicks his heels together with a snap. He carries a pointer)*

INVENTOR Highnesses! At your service!

GENERAL Tell these peasants what has happened to the world while they have been asleep in their committees.

INVENTOR *(The perfect schoolmaster)* I guessed that would be Your Highness' wishes! *(He claps his hands)* Lanterna magica! *(A screen descends from the top of the guillotine frame)* Take out your pens and papers, and don't copy from your neighbors! First slide, please!

(A slide appears. It shows an old-fashioned railway engine in motion. A gasp from the men)

14768 What's that?

INVENTOR I was expecting this question. This is a steam engine; this iron giant on two parallel rails can propel a thousand civilians or two thousand soldiers at sixty miles an hour.

71696 But where are the horses?

INVENTOR The horses are inside the boiler.
(*He begins to laugh*)

71696 Don't they get burned?
(*The* INVENTOR, *the* GENERAL *and the* ENEMY LEADER *laugh*)

INVENTOR Ach, it's too good! Next slide, please! (*A Victorian battleship appears. The men show consternation*) This is a dreadnought! A ship which can destroy a city of twenty thousand people in ten minutes with its guns. It travels fifteen sea miles in the hour thanks to its boilers. (*He points*) The steam escapes through the funnels.

35914 How does it work? Like a kettle?

INVENTOR (*Surprised*) This boy shows promise. Yes, like a huge kettle!

35914 Which blows the steam against the sails?
(*Great laughter*)

ENEMY LEADER Say what you will, the peasant is the salt of the earth!

INVENTOR (*Still laughing*) Next slide. (*An ancient airplane appears. The men panic*) This is an airplane, which can fly like a bird with as many as two men aboard for up to two hours!

94343 It flies? With men in it?

INVENTOR (*Pointing*) You can see the men clearly in the photograph.

GENERAL Well, Rebel?

REBEL If birds can fly, why shouldn't man? It was only

to be expected eventually. But who pays for all this progress?

INVENTOR Next slide. (*Some miserable children appear in a factory scene*) With child labor, production is rising, the market is booming. There never has been such prosperity in all of history!

REBEL You put children to work?

ENEMY LEADER Not just any children, working-class children. They know their station. They expect nothing else, and they are happy with their lot.

ARCHBISHOP They receive religious instruction?

GENERAL Free!

ARCHBISHOP That sounds like progress indeed.

INVENTOR It is not merely child labor, that is a detail! Next slide! (*A long row of native porters appears in a tropical setting*) We have empires on which the sun never sets, in which we have found unlimited resources beneath the soil and unlimited resources on the soil to drag those riches to the surface!

ENEMY LEADER Well, Rebel? Do you understand how feeble ideas are against resources?

REBEL It will not always be so. If the sun never sets on your empires, it follows that it never rises either. You will destroy your own prosperity out of force of habit. Rome did it. Summer does not last forever, and it is not spring which lies in wait for you, but autumn.

(*The men look at one another in perplexity*)

INVENTOR Next slide! (*A machine gun appears*) This is a machine gun, which can fire a hundred bullets in a minute, and kill as many men if correctly aimed!

94343 (*Suddenly, with devotion*) Long live their Highnesses!

(The ARCHBISHOP *launches himself eagerly into the fray)*

ARCHBISHOP Hip! Hip! Hip!

ALL 'Ray!

(A bugle sounds)

14768 There's the bugle, lads! Come on! At the double!

(The men exit)

REBEL *(To the* ARCHBISHOP*)* You, too?

(The REBEL *goes, quickly)*

ENEMY LEADER After him!

GENERAL Don't bother, Cousin. He has nowhere to go but the world, and that is shrinking.

ENEMY LEADER If it is shrinking as you say, we must have something to fear after all . . .

GENERAL Oh yes, dear Cousin . . . each other . . .

(They exit, laughing slightly. There is an explosion)

ARCHBISHOP What was that?

INVENTOR From the sound of it, it was a bomb. A home-made one.

(The REBEL *runs in and out. He stops when he hears the newspaperman)*

THE UNKNOWN SOLDIER Archduchess Carmensita assassinated! General mobilization! Read all about it!

ARCHBISHOP How was that? How ghastly! I'm afraid my money is rather out of date.

INVENTOR Here. Two papers, please.

ARCHBISHOP Who was the Archduchess Carmensita?

INVENTOR I don't know. There are so many of them. What interests me is the mobilization.

ARCHBISHOP (*Melancholy*) At moments, I feel we are like children who never grow up.

INVENTOR (*Sinister*) Thanks to me, the toys grow up instead.

(*They exit. The* WIFE *wanders on, dressed as a streetwalker*)

THE UNKNOWN SOLDIER Why d'you choose this pavement? D'you do it just to annoy me?

WIFE Annoy you? That's rich. I'm earning my living same as you are.

THE UNKNOWN SOLDIER There are plenty of other pavements. This is a big city.

WIFE That goes for you too.

THE UNKNOWN SOLDIER Aren't you ashamed of yourself?

WIFE Oh, how high and mighty we've become! What d'you think? I've been reduced to this before because of you. It's better than the workhouse. I can choose my own clothes, and I can sleep till noon.

THE UNKNOWN SOLDIER But what happens the rest of the time?

WIFE It's good for you to imagine. I've lived longer than you have, remember. I got to ninety-three one time, and I've reached eighty quite often. You're a quite small part of my life, come to think of it. I know your son much better than I'll ever know you.

THE UNKNOWN SOLDIER (*Bleak*) How is he?

WIFE Last time he was born blind and backward. The doctor said it must have been the shock of seeing you go.

(*The* SERGEANT *enters. He wears a black armband*)

THE UNKNOWN SOLDIER (*Horrified, miserable*) War declared! Read all about it! (*The* SERGEANT *buys a paper*)

Blind and backward!

SERGEANT Let's have the change, then! What's the matter with you?

THE UNKNOWN SOLDIER Sorry, mister.

SERGEANT You'll be in the army soon, my lad. That'll wake up your ideas for you! (*He looks at the paper*) War, eh? Just as well. I'll give it three weeks with all the modern weapons we got.

(*He exits*)

THE UNKNOWN SOLDIER Blind and backward? Well, that does it. I'm not going this time. I'm going to register as a conscientious objector.

WIFE You? (*she laughs*) Isn't it marvelous. My lad a conshie!

THE UNKNOWN SOLDIER Well, I might as well be for all the use I am. In all these thousands of years, I've never killed anyone. I only go out there in order to get killed. You're right. It's silly.

WIFE D'you expect me—or anyone else for that matter, to look up to you if you don't go do your bit?

THE UNKNOWN SOLDIER My bit? What the hell are you talking about? I want to stay with you for a change. I want to see the boy!

WIFE There isn't no boy, and there won't be another one if I can help it.

THE UNKNOWN SOLDIER Then why are you so keen for me to go, if you don't care for me?

WIFE (*Irritated*) Oh, you know us, surely, after all this time. In spite of all my good resolutions, something always goes wrong sooner or later. I find myself that way.

THE UNKNOWN SOLDIER It may be someone else this time.

WIFE (*Hotly*) Someone else? What do you take me for? (35914 *enters as a working-man*) Hello, honey.

35914 Sorry, no time now. Going to join up! See you when I come back on leave.

THE UNKNOWN SOLDIER Read all about it!

35914 (*Cheerful*) I've had all the bad news I can take for one day.

(*He exits*)

WIFE There's a real man.

THE UNKNOWN SOLDIER I don't understand you any more.

WIFE Think of the neighbors if we hitch up again. How can I hold up my head if everyone knows my husband's a coward?

THE UNKNOWN SOLDIER Oh, we've got neighbors now?

WIFE The world's much fuller than it was. People talk. From balconies, on the stairs, in the shops. They come in to borrow things, without knocking. There's no private life no more. That's why I want you to go, dear. Only don't volunteer for nothing this time. I want you back, d'you hear me? Keep your head down. Be the last over the top, dear.

(*The* SOLDIERS *pass—all dressed as civilians, but with rifles and suitcases. The* SERGEANT *leads the way*)

ALL (*Singing; very sentimental*)
Every hour, round the clock
I will think of you,
If every hour, round the clock
You will think of me.

Every key must fit a lock,
And every lock a key.
My key's lock is only you,
If your lock's key is me.
(They exit)

WIFE *(In tears)* Give your son a dad to be proud of!
(They kiss passionately)

THE UNKNOWN SOLDIER Wait for me, lads!
(The WIFE *follows slowly, waving her little handkerchief and wiping her tears. The* GENERAL *wanders on, in a bad humor. He is in khaki. The* INVENTOR *follows him. He is in a lab coat)*

INVENTOR I think I have something at last, Your Highness.

GENERAL You think you have something? You *think*? Great God almighty, Professor, three Christmases have come and gone, and still we have found no low trick with which to break the enemy's resistance.

INVENTOR We have had to stop work from time to time, Your Highness, to improvise counter-measures to his new weapons.

GENERAL How does he get all the new weapons before us, Professor?

INVENTOR That is the luck of the game, Your Highness.

GENERAL Game, man? You call it a game when all we stand for could be brushed aside in a minute? We might even be forced to spend the remainder of our days in exile—do you realize that? Archduke of nothing more than a floor in a four-star hotel!

INVENTOR *(Piqued)* If you don't want my invention, I can easily take it elsewhere.

GENERAL Good gracious me, no. Can't you understand a joke?

INVENTOR I can understand a joke which makes me laugh. Yours does not!

GENERAL What is this invention of yours?

INVENTOR Never mind.

GENERAL Now you're sulking again. Oh dear. What d'you want, a title? Sandwich?

INVENTOR A title? Sandwich?

GENERAL We'll make you a baron if this invention works.

INVENTOR What's the use of being a baron when I'm a genius?

GENERAL We realize that . . .

INVENTOR Whatever you give me, it will only be a fraction of what I can take whenever I want it!
(*He sways*)

GENERAL I realize that, Baron Schinkelmann.

INVENTOR I don't know what came over me. I have not slept for weeks, working on this confounded invention.

GENERAL Nobody is more conscious of your patriotism than we. Now, let's hear about it, Baron Schinkelmann.

INVENTOR I don't know how to thank you, Your Highness. You do me too great an honor.

GENERAL It will be the first of many if you bring us victory.

INVENTOR I have invented a new poison gas, Your Highness. No gas mask known to man can stand up against it. It pollutes crops, food, kills livestock, destroys everything it comes into contact with. It is lethal. That is why I have called it Lethanol.

GENERAL (*Smiling*) Why not Schinkelmannol?

INVENTOR (*With dignity*) Your Highness, I also invented the hypodermic needle and the safety pin. I have no wish to be remembered by a gas.

GENERAL When can we have this?

INVENTOR By Christmas.

GENERAL Not before?

INVENTOR By Christmas.

GENERAL Very well. Not a word to the Archbishop, is that understood?

INVENTOR Of course not, Your Highness.

GENERAL We are well satisfied, Baron. To work, to work. (*The* INVENTOR *clicks his heels, bows, and walks out. The* GENERAL *goes his way. Since the beginning of their scene, the stage has been growing darker, lit by occasional flashes. The* SOLDIERS *have been creeping onto the stage, their rifles cradled in their arms*)

94343 71696!

71696 What?

94343 We can't go no further than this. It's suicide!

14768 Sergeant isn't even here. He's gone sick again.

71696 Fact he ain't here don't make no difference to our orders.

35914 You make me puke, 71696. Ever since you got the bronze victory medal, you've been a public danger.

94343 Sah! Listen. (*From far away, we can hear a ragged male choir singing* "O Tannenbaum") It's the enemy.

35914 (*Glum*) Yeah. That reminds me. A merry Christmas, everyone.

ALL A merry Christmas.

(THE UNKNOWN SOLDIER *crawls forward with a tiny twig*)

14768 What you got here?

THE UNKNOWN SOLDIER Christmas tree. (*Laughter*) Sergeant's coming up, boys.

(*Everyone groans*)

SERGEANT Right. Break off the advance. There's something big in the air.

35914 Something new. (*Suddenly there is a strange tearing note, and a report*) That's it, lads! That was one of our shells. Didn't sound like a normal one to me.

94343 Listen! They've stopped singin'.

SERGEANT 654321987

THE UNKNOWN SOLDIER Yes, Sar'nt.

SERGEANT Lift yer head up, and see what that was.

35914 Don't be a fool!

THE UNKNOWN SOLDIER (*Half looking up*) That's odd. Looks like a smoke screen.

SERGEANT Can't be a shiftin' smoke screen if we're not going into the attack, you dollop.

THE UNKNOWN SOLDIER That's what it looks like. It's white.

35914 Hey! Can you smell something?

94343 Yes, like lavender.

71696 More like a wet dog now.

35914 Yes, like a stale face-flannel.

14768 Like cats in a damp corridor.

SERGEANT It's gas! That's what it is!

(*There is general commotion and cries of "Gas!"*)

THE UNKNOWN SOLDIER (*Unconcerned*) Well, we'll soon know, because it's coming this way.

SERGEANT It's doin' what?

35914 (*Holding up his hand*) The wind! It's changed direction!

SERGEANT Put on your gas masks!

(*Before they have a chance to, they begin to cough, and the scene takes on the aspect of a weird, convulsive ballet. While it is still going on, the* GENERAL *walks on from one side, the* ENEMY LEADER *from the other*)

GENERAL Allow us to congratulate you.

ENEMY LEADER You had bad luck. If the wind hadn't changed, our positions would have been reversed.

GENERAL We have the honor of capitulating.

ENEMY LEADER We have the honor of returning your sword.

GENERAL No hard feelings?

ENEMY LEADER Of course not. It was fun while it lasted. What news from home?

GENERAL Revolution.

ENEMY LEADER Same with us.

GENERAL Will you be going into exile?

ENEMY LEADER Where else?

GENERAL We will see each other there then.

ENEMY LEADER We moved our fortune to a neutral country when the war didn't end that first Christmas.

GENERAL So did we! We really have too much in common to quarrel like this.

ENEMY LEADER We only quarrel in public, dear Cousin.

GENERAL You will think us a very poor host, I'm afraid. We still have several thousand bottles of champagne in which to toast your victory, but unfortunately there's nobody left to serve it . . .

(They walk off arm in arm. The lights come up, and the men are in their gas-capes again. They push the tomb back into place. The SERGEANT *walks on, exactly as he was in the beginning)*

SERGEANT All right! Everybody back into place as you was in the beginnin'. Move! Don't know what came over you all? Only a few minutes before we're on the air. Move!

(The ARCHBISHOP *rushes on)*

ARCHBISHOP What happened? I seemed to lose touch with you all.

SERGEANT We can go into that later, Your Grace. We've got a ceremony to get through now. *(The* WIFE *enters)* Ah, there you are, little lady, we'll have to decide what to do with you now, won't we? There's someone missin'. *(The* REBEL *enters)* Ah, it's you, yes. Late as usual. Lie down where you was, out of it.

(The GENERAL *enters, still adjusting his tie)*

GENERAL What hit us? It was like a sudden blackout. *(The* ENEMY LEADER *comes on, wearing a sheep-lined duffel coat)* What are you doing here? You were always my enemy before.

ENEMY LEADER *(Smiling)* Oh, that was long ago. But I still am your enemy in a way. I'm the director of the television coverage. I stand between you and your public. Every false note, every half-truth, and I magnify it out of all proportion, in color.

(*The* INVENTOR *comes on*)

INVENTOR (*Livid*) It's a scandal! This country calls itself a modern state, and my chauffeur can't even park my car in the V.I.P. enclosure because I haven't got a red sticker. (*Shouting*) I was never sent a red sticker! I have had to walk a mile through the crowd!

GENERAL (*Beginning to lose his head*) I'm very sorry, Professor, it's not my fault. I have to organize . . .

INVENTOR (*Furious*) Organize! Why don't you use my computers? I don't know why I stay here. Every week I have offers to go and work elsewhere, where they don't make mistakes! (*He breaks off, and mutters, as an echo*) Where they don't make mistakes . . .

(THE UNKNOWN SOLDIER *totters on, slowly and unsteadily. He is in tatters, and covered in blood. There is a petrified silence. The* WIFE *is the first to break it*)

WIFE Oh, my darling!

THE UNKNOWN SOLDIER (*Restrains her. He speaks with clarity, but it's clearly an effort*) Don't come near me . . . sweetheart . . . you'll get your clothes all dirty . . . and then, I'm only held together with bandages . . . if you touch me . . . I might fall apart . . .

SERGEANT (*Finding his tongue*) Why isn't you in yer coffin as per instructions?

THE UNKNOWN SOLDIER I decided . . . not to die this time.

SERGEANT Decided not to die? It's not for you to decide this, that, or the copulatin' other. You know yer orders!

THE UNKNOWN SOLDIER I decided . . . not to die.

GENERAL (*Shaken*) Is that quite fair? All the arrangements for your funeral have been made. You know that. In a few minutes, you'll be on television.

THE UNKNOWN SOLDIER I'm sorry, General. There it is.

ARCHBISHOP It is not given to everyone to have a ceremony as fine as this in his honor, you know . . . and it is in your honor.

THE UNKNOWN SOLDIER I came here . . . as quick as I could . . . and then I thought . . . what if I don't make it in time? They'll have their ceremony just the same . . . there's no need for a body . . . There's a lid on the coffin . . . there's never been no need for a body . . .

GENERAL Are you seriously suggesting we should cheat the public?

THE UNKNOWN SOLDIER You cheat the public every time you declare war. Why not now?

(*The* SERGEANT *runs amok*)

SERGEANT Let me get at 'im. Give me a rifle, someone. I'll finish 'im off. It won't take much!

(*The soldiers deny him their rifles, and struggle with him*)

GENERAL Sergeant! Sergeant!

(*The* SERGEANT suddenly goes limp)

SERGEANT (*Pathetic*) I can't go on, sir . . . I never seen the like . . . I'm givin' up, sir . . . I'm givin' . . . (*He tries to stand up*) Permission to . . .

(*He falls*)

THE UNKNOWN SOLDIER There. I've killed a man at last . . . there goes my clean sheet . . . after all this time. Sir?

GENERAL (*Upset*) Yes?

THE UNKNOWN SOLDIER May I make a suggestion?

GENERAL What is it?

THE UNKNOWN SOLDIER You've got an empty coffin,

haven't you . . . now you've got a corpse . . . what with the soldiers and the flags and the drums . . . he deserves it much more than I ever did.

GENERAL What do you say, Archbishop?

ARCHBISHOP Well, it's a little irregular. I mean, the sergeant was hardly unknown, was he?

WIFE (*Emotional*) My man wasn't unknown either. You all know him. You've known him for centuries. He's just known as the Unknown Soldier!

ARCHBISHOP Yes, that's quite true.

GENERAL Men, place the sergeant in the tomb.

(*The men begin to do so*)

ENEMY LEADER We have three minutes to go.

(*The* WIFE *grips her stomach and starts writhing*)

THE UNKNOWN SOLDIER What is it, doll?

WIFE It's started.

GENERAL Not here, for heaven's sake!

THE UNKNOWN SOLDIER I'm going to see my son!

(*A nurse enters. It is the* WOMAN)

GENERAL Take her away.

WOMAN It's too dangerous to move her now.

WIFE Oh. Your Highness.

WOMAN (*Gentle. Laying her down. The soldiers offer their greatcoats*) Yes. Her Highness. Doing something useful at last . . .

GENERAL But the ceremony? You'll have to keep the cameras away from this area.

ENEMY LEADER We shoot whatever's newsworthy.

ARCHBISHOP Am I to understand that my address to the nation . . .

ENEMY LEADER We try to give the public what it wants.

REBEL You see, this is the real revolution at last. The one man who has never changed, the one constant factor throughout history, has woken up.

INVENTOR Woken up? What are you talking about? A man has refused to die, that's all. What is so surprising about it?

REBEL He is in charge. We are awaiting his decision, awaiting his orders.

INVENTOR I am not awaiting his orders! The next time you will all be unknown soldiers, I have seen to that! This man is incapable of decision! It is I who can destroy the world!

REBEL He can prevent you.

INVENTOR I can order him to press the button!

REBEL He can refuse.

INVENTOR I am a genius! I harness the power of the earth and sky!

REBEL He is a simple man. He harnesses the imagination. (*The* WIFE *cries out*)

THE UNKNOWN SOLDIER Professor, you're an intelligent man . . . with all your knowledge . . . you must know something about childbirth.

INVENTOR I beg your pardon? Childbirth? (*He looks at the* WIFE *for the first time, as she lies, surrounded by a wall of soldiers*) Ach, you are doing it all wrong. You are not making it easy for her that way. Higher with the legs. Lower with the head. More pillows. Quick. Now give her one of these pills to suck. They are called Laborine. I invented them for just such an emergency . . .

ENEMY LEADER Five, four, three, two, one. We're on the air!

(The red light on the camera lights up)

ARCHBISHOP *(Amplified electronically)* Fellow countrymen. Who was the Unknown Soldier? Was he tall or short, fair or dark? We know not. Did he come from North or South, East or West? We know not. What was the color of his skin, what were his pleasures and his fears, his loves, his hatreds? We know not. All we know about him is that he died in battle as many others did, to defend his country and his religion, and our right to be free!

(A child starts crying fitfully. The soldiers form a little cluster around the WIFE. *The* ENEMY LEADER *looks up at the control room)*

ENEMY LEADER *(Sotto voce, but projected urgently)* All cameras concentrate on the childbirth—cut off the Archbishop's mike!

ARCHBISHOP Let us then reflect, our hands on our hearts, our eyes on the . . .

(He continues his speech, in silence)

INVENTOR Easy! Easy, nurse! So . . . let nature take its course! Good! . . . Nature is doing surprisingly well, all by itself! . . . So . . . so . . . It works!

(The child begins to wail. THE UNKNOWN SOLDIER *begins to laugh incredulously. His delight is contagious. The* ARCHBISHOP *goes on obliviously with his silent invocation to the nation. Suddenly a siren sounds. Panic. Only the* ARCHBISHOP *is too wrapped up in what he is saying to notice)*

REBEL What is it?

INVENTOR *(Hysterical)* I gave no order!

94343 What is it then?

71696 The balloon goin' up, I wouldn't be surprised.

35914 It may only be a factory . . . on a time signal . . . or the fire department!

14768 Listen!

(There is silence, except for the child's crying)

INVENTOR There is no use listening! We will never hear it coming . . . are you completely heartless! To interrupt a childbirth?

GENERAL What is it, Professor? As commander-in-chief, I deserve to know.

INVENTOR It may be the enemy.

GENERAL I knew we should have attacked him first!

INVENTOR It may be a short-circuit in the early warning system . . . it may be a short-circuit in the system warning us of a short circuit in the early warning system . . . it could be almost anything, ad infinitum, et cetera . . .

GENERAL Right! Where's the Sergeant?

REBEL He's dead for good this time . . . there's no place for him in a society advanced enough to destroy itself.

(THE UNKNOWN SOLDIER *appears with the child in his arms*)

GENERAL Right. Form up. Put down that child, man.

REBEL (*To* THE UNKNOWN SOLDIER) You lead us!

(Enthusiasm from the men)

GENERAL That's rank disobedience!

REBEL Look where centuries of obedience has got us!

THE UNKNOWN SOLDIER Come then, my darling. Well, there's nowhere left to hide, lads . . . I reckon the only way to go is out in the open. If we don't find an enemy to share our common interests . . . then we don't deserve to survive . . .

35914 Common interests . . . flowers?

THE UNKNOWN SOLDIER No . . . living this time.

ENEMY LEADER *(To the audience)* Normal service will be resumed after this message . . .

(The lights fade on the still garrulous ARCHBISHOP*)*

THE UNKNOWN SOLDIER *(With a sad smile to the audience, who are suddenly lit up)* Well, don't expect me to do everything just because I'm not dead. It's up to you too, all of you. Come on, lads . . .

(He leads his men out through the auditorium. The sirens grow in volume)

The End